The Transforming
Metropolitan
Economy

THOMAS M. STANBACK, JR., is professor emeritus at
New York University, where he taught from 1956 until
1986. He also served as senior research associate at the
Eisenhower Center for the Conservation of Human
Resources, Columbia University, from 1963 to 2000.
His publications include *Suburbanization and the City;
The Economic Transformation of American Cities* and *Cities
in Transformation* (with Thierry Noyelle); and *Services,
The New Economy* (with Peter Bearse, Thierry Noyelle,
and Robert Karasek).

The Transforming Metropolitan Economy

THOMAS M. STANBACK, Jr.

with the assistance of Gregory Grove

CENTER FOR URBAN POLICY RESEARCH
EDWARD J. BLOUSTEIN SCHOOL OF PLANNING AND PUBLIC POLICY
RUTGERS, THE STATE UNIVERSITY OF NEW JERSEY
NEW BRUNSWICK, NEW JERSEY

Published by the Center for Urban Policy Research
Edward J. Bloustein School of Planning and Public Policy
Rutgers, The State University of New Jersey
Civic Square • 33 Livingston Avenue
New Brunswick, New Jersey 08901-1982

Printed in the United States of America

Library of Congress Cataloging-in-Publication Data

Stanback, Thomas M.
    The transforming metropolitan economy / Thomas M. Stanback, Jr. with
the assistance of Gregory Grove.
        p.   cm.
    Includes bibliographical references.
    ISBN 0-88285-173-X (pbk. : alk. paper)

    1. Metropolitan areas—United States.   2. United States—Economic
conditions—1971–1981. 3. United States—Economic conditions—1981– I. Grove,
Gregory. II. Title.

HT334.U5 S73 2002
330.973'009173'2—dc21   2001047403

Cover design: Helene Berinsky

Contents

Tables

Foreword

It is with much pride and pleasure that I write the foreword to Thomas Stanback's most recently completed study, *The Transforming Metropolitan Economy, 1974–1997*. I met Professor Stanback for the first time in the early 1960s, was greatly impressed with his interest in and focus on urban economics, and suggested that he shift his research affiliation, while maintaining his faculty post at New York University, from the National Bureau of Economic Research to our Columbia University Conservation of Human Resources Project, to head up our urban research. He accepted the offer, and during the succeeding decades, with the cooperation of a stellar group of younger urban scholars including Richard Knight, Robert Cohen, Matthew Drennan, Roger Waldinger, and Thierry Noyelle, he and his associates produced a considerable number of critical studies that greatly advanced our understanding of the transformations under way in the metropolitan areas of the United States. As the twenty-first century begins, these metropolitan areas now account for more than 80 percent of the total U.S. population and are the source of an even higher percentage of the nation's annual gross domestic product.

A careful reading of Stanback's book alerted me, among other findings, to the following, about which I earlier had little awareness: the radical decline of the manufacturing sector, with a corresponding explosion of business and professional services and of the nonprofit sector. But Stanback also calls attention to several transformations in the U.S. economy during the last quarter of the twentieth century, among the most important of which is the growing importance of "non-earned income"—dividends, interest, and rent payments, as well as transfer payments—in the changing composition of the nation's annual output.

Another major contribution of Stanback's latest volume is his careful analysis of the continuities as well as the changes that have occurred among metropolitan economies of different sizes and specialization. While the "nodal" metropolitan centers with two million or more population, such as New York, Philadelphia, and Boston in the East; Los Angeles, Phoenix, Chicago, and the Twin Cities in the Midwest and West; and Houston, Atlanta, and Dallas in the South have profited both in their rapid growth and diversity, some of the nodal centers with less population growth have enjoyed more rapid rates of income growth during the last twenty-five years of the twentieth century.

I want to thank Tom Stanback for the quality of his research in terms of the important questions that he has raised and answered and for the lucidity of his writing and the clarity with which his proposed findings emerge. No one who is interested in and concerned with the next stages in the evolution of the highly dynamic U.S. economy as it entered the twenty-first century can fail to be impressed by a close reading of Stanback's rich and incisive analysis.

ELI GINZBERG
Hepburn Professor Emeritus of Economics
Eisenhower Center for the Conservation of Human Resources
Columbia Business School
Columbia University
New York, New York

Acknowledgments

My greatest debt is to Gregory Grove, who assisted me in the data analysis and preparation of tables from the very beginning of this project until its conclusion. Sergei Tikhonov was responsible for the initial programming of the 1974 and 1990 county data, Cheolwon Ryu for the subsequent programming of the (revised) 1974 and 1990 county data, and Mark Topping for preparing preliminary tables from the BEA materials. Thierry Noyelle, Alex Schwartz, and John McDonald offered valuable suggestions in the early months of the study. My special thanks go to Eli Ginzberg and Matthew Drennan for their reading of the manuscript at several stages and for their encouragement throughout. Finally, I wish to thank Shoshana Vasheetz for her patience and skill in typing the manuscript in its various revisions.

1

An Era of Metropolitan Transformation: 1974–1997

The postwar years have been marked by the decline of goods-producing sectors as providers of jobs in the U.S. economy and by the continuous rise in importance of most service sectors. This shift toward services has touched every city, town, and hamlet in the country. Yet the impact of this transformation on employment, earnings, and income has varied widely among places, affecting their chances for prosperity and a favorable employment environment in the years ahead.

It is the principal task of this study to examine, across the full spectrum of continental U.S. metropolitan areas (hereafter, "metros"), the extent to which these economies varied in rates and patterns of growth in employment, earnings, and income, as well as in the industrial composition of employment, during the period 1974–97.

By focusing on the metropolitan area rather than only the central city, the study recognizes that suburbs have become more than hinterland markets or sources of commuter labor for the central city. Rather, suburb and central city are closely and symbiotically related economically—and, to a significant degree, culturally as well. The metropolitan area—the central city and outlying suburban areas combined—provides an appropriate unit of analysis for examining the current urban system of the United States.

Nature and Scope of the Study

This study is a sequel to *The Economic Transformation of American Cities*.[1] Like its predecessor, its principal objectives are to distinguish among metropolitan areas in terms of their industrial specialization and to determine how changes in the U.S. economy are influencing their industrial composition and their prospects for future development. (For a definition of metros and a discussion of data sources and methodology, see appendix A.)

The study differs from *The Economic Transformation of American Cities* in two important ways. First, it relies almost entirely on data collected and published by the U.S. government, whereas the earlier study drew upon analysis both of government data and of varied information drawn from directories and business and government publications. Second, it is broader in certain respects:

1. It covers all sizes of metros in the continental United States rather than being confined to those with more than 250,000 in population.
2. It analyzes not only employment data for each metro, but also earnings data and data for non-earned income (dividends, interest, and rent payments, or DIR; and transfer payments, or TP).
3. It makes use of a format of industrial categories and subcategories (see table 1.3 below) that provides somewhat greater detail than did the industry breakdown used in the earlier study.[2]

Key Observations

Before undertaking this analysis, it is useful to set forth under five headings some key observations about the metropolitan economies of the United States:

1. The increasing importance of services as a source of job creation
2. The dominant role of metropolitan economies
3. Highlights from the classification analysis—by economic specialization and population size—of the U.S. metropolitan system
4. The wide-ranging differences in patterns of growth in employment, earnings, and income among metropolitan areas
5. The increased importance of non-earned income as a source of aggregate demand within metropolitan economies.

The Shift to Services

Table 1.1 makes clear that changes in the industrial composition of employment during the years covered by the present study were largely a continuation of trends extending back to the early postwar years. During that period, major losses occurred in the shares of total U.S. employment accounted for by goods production, and major gains were made in the shares of several of the service categories, especially the large catchall classification, "services," which includes health services, business/professional services, social/organizational services, and consumer services.

TABLE 1.1

Distribution (Percentage) of U.S. Nonfarm Employment among Industry Categories, 1950–97

Industrial Category	1950	1960	1970	1974	1990	1997
Mining	1.99	1.31	0.88	0.89	0.65	0.48
Construction	5.21	5.32	4.99	5.05	4.68	4.63
Manufacturing	33.45	30.97	27.28	25.56	17.41	15.21
Transportation, Communications, and Utilities	8.89	7.38	6.35	5.99	5.29	5.21
Wholesale Trade	} 21.56	5.54	5.38	5.39	5.65	5.42
Retail Trade		15.46	15.83	16.32	17.92	17.94
Finance, Insurance, and Real Estate (FIRE)	4.08	4.92	5.20	5.37	6.13	5.78
Services	11.35	13.69	16.39	17.37	25.60	29.37
Government						
Federal (including Military)	N.A.	4.19	3.85	3.47	2.81	2.20
State and Local	N.A.	11.21	13.86	14.61	13.86	13.75
Total	100.00	100.00	100.00	100.00	100.00	100.00

Note: N. A. = not available.

Source: U.S. Bureau of Labor Statistics.

The Two Periods: 1974–90 and 1990–97

In much of the analysis, the years from 1974 to 1997 are broken into two subperiods: 1974–90 and 1990–97. The initial year selected for study is 1974 because it roughly coincides with the beginning of an era for the U.S. economy that many economists designate as sharply different from the preceding one. During most of this new period, real wages declined or ceased to grow, inequality increased within the system, and the economy was characterized by deindustrialization. At the same time, there was greater globalization of production and trade. Toward the late 1980s, however, declines in productivity gave way to a leveling off, followed in the early 1990s by a period of rising productivity and vigorous prosperity that continued through the early months of the twenty-first century.

Curiously, the subperiod 1990–97 was marked by lower rates of growth in U.S. employment than was the subperiod 1974–90 (table 1.2). The explanation for this paradox appears to lie largely in the record-breaking increases in the numbers of women entering the labor force during the 1970s and 1980s in comparison with lesser rates of increase during the 1990s. In 1970, the labor force participation rate for women stood at 43.3 percent and the ratio of employment to population at 40.8 percent. In 1990, the corresponding rates were 57.5 and 54.3 percent (increases of 14.3 and 13.5 percentage points). By 1997, these rates had advanced to 59.8 and 56.8 percent (gains of 2.4 and 5.5 percentage points).

Highlights of Employment Change, 1974–90 and 1990–97

Measures highlighting the overall U.S. experience for the periods studied are presented in table 1.2. The distribution of employment among industrial categories and subcategories in 1974, 1990, and 1997 is shown alongside annualized rates of change for 1974–90 and 1990–97 and shares of total job increases during the two periods. Employment in all three goods categories (mining, construction, and manufacturing) declined in relative importance (i.e., in share of employment) during the entire 23 years, as did transportation, communications, and utilities (TCU); wholesaling; and the federal government, the military, and state and local government. Only in manufacturing, however, was there a net decline in jobs. Among the remaining categories—all service activities—shares of employment increased, some quite dramatically.

The shares (i.e., distribution) of job increases, however, show most clearly the major sources of job growth.[3] From 1974 to 1990, retailing, with 15.5 percent of nonfarm employment in 1974, accounted for 21.6 percent of net job increases; business/professional services and non-profit services, with combined shares of 11.5 percent of 1974 employment, accounted for an astounding 40.3 percent of net job increases. The remaining net job increases were accounted for largely by government (9.7 percent); finance, insurance, and real estate, or FIRE (7.6 percent); wholesale trade (5.5 percent); and TCU (4.5 percent).

During the 1990s, job increases were dominated by business/professional services (25.4 percent) and nonprofit services (27.2 percent), whereas retailing and FIRE accounted for sharply reduced shares (15.6 and 2.9 percent, respectively). State and local government's share of job increases (11.1 percent) was the remaining important contributor to employment growth.

The 1974–90 data for annualized rates of change given in table 1.2 show once again the very wide variation in employment growth among the service categories, ranging from 7.0 percent for business/professional services and 5.6 percent for health services to less than 1 percent for federal government and military employment and a negative rate of 0.4 percent for the large manufacturing sector. During the 1990–97 period, rates for all industrial categories were lower. But once again, business/professional and health services grew most rapidly; and manufacturing and the federal government and military, the least. One of the sharpest declines in the rate of employment growth occurred in the financial sector: from an annualized rate of 3.0 percent during the first period to well under 1 percent (0.8 percent) in the second.

The Dominant Role of Metropolitan Economies

In large measure, this shift toward increased service employment in the United States has been associated with the growth of metropolitan economies.[4] This is true both because metros have accounted for the large majority of nonfarm employment in the United States (80.8 percent in 1974; 82.5 percent in 1997) and because service employment accounts for a larger share of jobs in metros than in nonmetro counties (table 1.3).

TABLE 1.2

Distribution of U.S. Nonfarm Employment among Industrial Categories, 1974, 1990, and 1997;
Distribution of Job Increases, 1974–90 and 1990–97; and Rates of Change (annualized), 1974–90 and 1990–1997

Industrial Category	Share of Employment (percentage)			Share of Job Increases (percentage)		Annualized Rate of Change	
	1974	1990	1997	1974–90	1990–97	1974–90	1990–97
Mining	0.85	0.64	0.47	0.14	*	0.42	-2.95
Construction	4.95	4.62	4.38	3.74	1.95	1.76	0.73
Manufacturing	25.47	16.89	14.81	*	*	-0.38	-0.41
Transportation, Communications, and Utilities	5.07	4.93	4.96	4.49	4.68	2.03	1.59
Wholesale Trade	5.56	5.57	5.41	5.48	3.45	2.22	1.06
Retail Trade	15.51	17.46	17.49	21.63	15.62	2.97	1.51
Finance, Insurance, and Real Estate (FIRE)	5.43	6.13	5.85	7.63	2.93	2.98	0.82
Business/Professional Services	3.69	7.67	9.75	16.80	25.45	6.98	5.02
Nonprofit Services	7.80	12.57	14.37	23.46	27.17	5.31	3.43
Health Services	4.61	7.76	9.02	14.96	18.12	5.59	3.68
Educational Services	1.18	1.55	1.74	2.37	3.06	3.96	3.17
Social Services/Organizations	2.01	3.26	3.61	6.13	5.99	5.35	2.96
Consumer Services	3.88	4.82	5.20	6.89	7.64	3.59	2.58
Government/Services							
Federal	3.63	2.85	2.24	0.87	*	0.61	-1.98
Military	3.42	2.42	1.72	0.08	*	0.07	-3.36
State and Local	14.74	13.43	13.35	8.78	11.11	1.43	1.40
Total	100.00	100.00	100.00	100.00	100.00	2.18	1.48
Administration/Auxiliary	2.83	3.11	2.64	3.70	*	2.81	-0.85

Note: An asterisk indicates that employment decreased.

Source: County Business Patterns. Data for Government Services is from the U.S. Bureau of Economic Analysis.

TABLE 1.3

Distribution of U.S. Nonfarm Employment among Industrial Categories and Location Quotients,
All Metros and Non-Metro Counties, 1974, 1990, and 1997

Industrial Category	U.S. Distribution (percentage)			Location Quotients					
				All Metros			Non-Metro Counties		
	1974	1990	1997	1974	1990	1997	1974	1990	1997
Mining	0.85	0.64	0.47	0.55	0.57	0.60	2.92	3.10	2.89
Construction	4.95	4.62	4.38	1.04	1.03	1.01	0.84	0.87	0.94
Manufacturing	25.47	16.89	14.81	0.96	0.93	0.91	1.16	1.34	1.41
Transportation, Communications, and Utilities	5.07	4.93	4.96	1.07	1.04	1.05	0.68	0.79	0.77
Transportation	2.67	2.75	3.02	1.09	1.06	1.06	0.60	0.72	0.74
Communications and Utilities	2.27	1.89	1.79	1.04	1.01	1.03	0.82	0.97	0.87
Wholesale Trade	5.56	5.57	5.41	1.05	1.05	1.06	0.79	0.73	0.70
Retail Trade	15.51	17.46	17.49	1.00	0.99	0.99	1.00	1.05	1.07
Finance, Insurance, and Real Estate (FIRE)	5.43	6.13	5.85	1.10	1.09	1.10	0.57	0.57	0.55
Banking/Credit Agencies	2.05	2.24	2.09	1.03	1.03	1.04	0.86	0.84	0.80
Insurance Carriers	1.40	1.24	1.24	1.18	1.14	1.16	0.25	0.32	0.22
FIRE Agents and Brokers	1.91	2.43	2.45	1.10	1.10	1.10	0.57	0.49	0.52
Business/Professional Services	3.69	7.67	9.75	1.14	1.13	1.12	0.39	0.38	0.41
Nonprofit Services	7.80	12.57	14.37	1.02	1.02	1.01	0.92	0.91	0.97
Health Services	4.61	7.76	9.02	1.02	1.02	1.00	0.90	0.92	1.02
Educational Services	1.18	1.55	1.74	1.06	1.06	1.06	0.76	0.71	0.72
Social Services/Organizations	2.01	3.26	3.61	0.99	1.00	1.01	1.05	0.99	0.97
Consumer Services	3.88	4.82	5.20	1.01	1.03	1.02	0.96	0.84	0.88
Government/Services	21.78	18.71	17.31	0.96	0.95	0.95	1.15	1.24	1.25
Federal	3.63	2.85	2.24	1.05	1.04	1.04	0.79	0.81	0.80
Military	3.42	2.42	1.72	0.98	0.98	0.98	1.11	1.11	1.09
State and Local	14.74	13.43	13.35	0.94	0.93	0.93	1.25	1.36	1.34
Total	100.00	100.00	100.00	100.00	100.00	100.00	100.00	100.00	100.00
Administration/Auxiliary	2.83	3.11	2.64	1.12	1.15	1.14	0.50	0.27	0.32
				Share of Total U.S. Employment (percentage)					
				80.80	83.20	82.53	19.20	16.80	17.47

Source: County Business Patterns. Data for Government Services is from the U.S. Bureau of Economic Analysis.

The essential difference between metros and nonmetro counties as regards the distribution of employment among industrial categories is readily seen by the comparison of location quotients (LQs) presented in table 1.3. LQs are simply indexes indicating the extent to which a given industry in a given place is overrepresented or underrepresented in employment relative to the United States as a whole. The measure is based on a comparison of the share of total employment accounted for by a given industry group in a given place with the comparable share of employment in the United States. Thus, in 1997 wholesaling accounted for 5.73 percent of total employment in metros relative to 5.41 percent in the nation as a whole. The resulting LQ is 1.06 (5.73 divided by 5.41).

On the basis of this measure, metros may be said to be overrepresented in wholesaling in 1990. In contrast, the 1997 LQ for wholesaling in nonmetro counties is 0.70. On average, employment in metros is clearly more concentrated in wholesaling than in nonmetro counties.

The LQs show that, for the United States as a whole, nonmetro counties are more heavily specialized in manufacturing than are metros.[5] Moreover, as manufacturing employment declined as a *share* of total U.S. employment during the period 1974–97, the *relative* importance of manufacturing increased in nonmetro counties (i.e., the LQ rose).

Table 1.3 also reveals the extent to which service employment is concentrated in metros. The greatest contrast is found in FIRE, business/professional services, and administration/auxiliary (A/A)—with respective metro LQs in 1997 of 1.10, 1.12, and 1.14, relative to 0.55, 0.41, and 0.32 for nonmetro counties. LQs are also higher for wholesaling, consumer services, and nonprofit services (although not for the subcategory social/organization services). These higher LQs indicate greater concentration of employment in these industrial categories. In government, however, the comparisons show a mixed experience: The LQ for federal employment is higher among metros; for military and state and local government employment (which includes employment in state universities), it is higher for nonmetro counties.

Furthermore, among the services that grew fastest in the United States as a whole (table 1.4), growth was relatively rapid—not only among metros, but among nonmetros as well. For example, in business/professional services and nonprofit services, high rates of growth in nonmetro counties buoyed low 1974 LQs to somewhat higher levels in 1997 (e.g., the business/professional services LQ rose from 0.39 to 0.41 and the nonprofit services LQ from 0.92 to 0.97).[6]

Clearly, the movement toward increasing importance for services has extended to all levels of the economy. This is true for at least two reasons. First, individuals everywhere in their roles as consumers make more and more use of a variety of services obtained at the local level (e.g., banking, income tax preparation, property leasing, pest control, education, and medical care). Second, many of these services have become a part of the local infrastructure serving businesses, institutions, and professional offices of all sizes.

TABLE 1.4

Rates of U.S. Employment Change by Industrial Category, Metro and Non-Metro Counties, 1974–90 and 1990–97 (percentage)

Industrial Category	United States		All Metros		Non-Metro Counties	
	1974–90	1990–97	1974–90	1990–97	1974–90	1990–97
Mining	0.42	-2.95	0.74	-2.49	0.15	-3.40
Construction	1.76	0.73	1.72	0.41	1.98	2.48
Manufacturing	-0.38	-0.41	-0.53	-0.80	0.13	0.87
Transportation, Communications, and Utilities	2.03	1.59	1.89	1.56	2.93	1.82
Transportation	2.40	2.86	2.26	2.73	3.44	3.77
Communications and Utilities	1.04	0.71	0.81	0.88	2.17	-0.20
Wholesale Trade	2.22	1.06	2.32	1.06	1.63	1.00
Retail Trade	2.97	1.51	2.92	1.32	3.16	2.35
Finance, Insurance, and Real Estate (FIRE)	2.98	0.82	2.94	0.82	3.36	0.82
Banking/Credit Agencies	2.76	0.53	2.79	0.53	2.57	0.51
Insurance Carriers	1.45	1.50	1.31	1.72	3.79	-3.05
FIRE Agents and Brokers	3.77	1.58	3.82	1.47	3.39	2.78
Business/Professional Services	6.98	5.02	6.79	4.88	9.04	6.98
Nonprofit Services	5.31	3.43	5.25	3.16	5.54	4.89
Health Services	5.59	3.68	5.58	3.27	5.64	5.75
Educational Services	3.96	3.17	3.68	3.08	5.45	3.82
Social Services/Organizations	5.35	2.96	5.35	2.90	5.39	3.22
Consumer Services	3.59	2.58	3.74	2.35	2.90	3.96
Government/Services	1.10	0.36	1.10	0.19	1.09	1.02
Federal	0.61	-1.98	0.61	-2.04	0.60	-1.61
Military	0.70	-3.36	0.10	-3.42	-0.06	-3.09
State and Local	1.43	1.40	1.45	1.26	1.37	1.85
Total	2.18	1.48	2.21	1.37	2.06	2.05
Administration/Auxiliary	2.81	-0.85	2.92	-1.00	1.66	2.01

Source: County Business Patterns.

Not only has the variety of banking services become greater (and more carefully tailored to the needs of smaller businesses and institutions), but a large number of freestanding business services (e.g., bookkeeping and taxes, computer programming and maintenance, building upkeep, credit reporting, and personnel supply) have become more attractive and affordable as an alternative to carrying out these functions *within* organizations everywhere, including small businesses.

In interpreting these findings, it is important to keep in mind that the industrial categories shown may include a fairly wide range of activities. This is readily observed in appendix B, which presents the detailed industrial classifications within the principal service categories. Thus the category banking/credit agencies includes both fairly routine retail banking activities but also the great banks of New York and other major banking centers, which serve not only the needs of the local population and business community but also "export" sophisticated banking services to large corporations and institutions and to small banks in distant places. The same is true of a variety of services—including insurance, engineering, investment, education, medical care, and government in a number of metros, as we shall see. Where such services are provided in excess of local requirements, the share of resources may be expected to be larger than average, and accordingly there will be an above-average share of employment.

Highlights of Metro Classification Analysis

A fundamental aspect of any analysis of growth and change within the U.S. metropolitan system is a recognition of the importance of both population size and economic specialization. Small places do not play the same role within the national economy as do large places and may not be expected to respond in the same way to major economic forces. Similarly, urban economies vary in economic specialization, even within the same size class (e.g., some metros specialize in manufacturing, some in finance and commerce, and some in resort amenities). Moreover, the degree and nature of such specialization may be expected to affect the composition of the workforce and the pattern of growth and development.

In this study, metropolitan areas have been classified according to economic specialization in 1990 and broken down further by size.[7] The results of the classification are presented in chapter 2. Table 1.5 presents the number of metros in each type/size group discussed in chapter 2 and the percentage of total metropolitan employment accounted for by each.

An initial finding is that the larger metros account for a major share of total employment: The 170 largest metros (those with a population of 250,000 or more in 1990), which make up roughly half of all metropolitan economies, accounted for 90 percent of all metropolitan employment in 1997. Moreover, employment is heavily concentrated at the top of the hierarchy. The 21 largest metros (those with 2 million or more population) account for slightly more than 40 percent of metropolitan employment.

TABLE 1.5
Number of Metros and Percentage of Metro Employment, by Type and Population, 1997

Type of Metro	Number of Metros	Metro Population			
		> 2 Million	1–2 Million	250,000–1 Million	< 250,000
Nodal	88	16	18	22	32
Functional Nodal	22	1	3	13	5
Manufacturing/Service	56	0	0	12	44
Manufacturing	27	0	0	22	5
Government/Service	62	1	1	31	29
Government/Military	37	1	2	13	21
Resort/Retirement	25	2	2	9	12
Unclassified[a]	2	0	0	1	1
Total	319	21	26	123	149

Type of Metro	Total	Percentage of Metro Employment			
		> 2 Million	1–2 Million	250,000–1 Million	< 250,000
Nodal	55.7	32.6	14.8	6.0	2.2
Functional Nodal	8.2	2.0	2.6	3.4	0.3
Manufacturing/Service	5.6	0.0	0.0	2.8	2.8
Manufacturing	4.3	0.0	0.0	3.7	0.6
Government/Service	13.1	2.4	1.7	6.9	2.2
Government/Military	6.1	1.2	1.4	2.1	1.3
Resort/Retirement	6.4	2.0	2.3	1.4	0.7
Unclassified[a]	6.0	0.0	0.0	0.6	0.0
Total	100.0	40.2	22.7	27.0	10.1

Note: a. Includes Honolulu, HI, and Anchorage, AK.
Source: County Business Patterns.

A second finding is that those metros classified as *diversified service*, or *nodal*, centers account for a large majority of metropolitan employment—about 56 percent—and that the 16 largest nodal metros (those with more than 2 million population) account for 33 percent. In chapter 2, we shall see that, although the nodal metros are metropolitan places with relatively high concentrations in several service categories (principally commercial and/or financial), the remaining metros are more narrowly specialized. Three types of these *specialized metros* are oriented principally toward manufacturing: *functional nodal places*, metros with a strong headquarters presence as well as a strong industrial specialization; *manufacturing/service metros*, manufacturing economies with a significant specialization in services; and *manufacturing metros*, places characterized by heavy specialization in manufacturing with relatively few services. The remaining types are *government/service metros*, which tend to be specialized as state capitals and/ or as sites of state-operated universities and medical centers; *government/military metros*, sites of military or other government installations; and *resort/retirement metros*, places heavily specialized as resorts or as meccas for retired persons.

Differing Patterns of Growth

Table 1.6 indicates a considerable range of experience among type/size groups of metros, both as regards employment growth and rates of change in earnings and income. The table also reveals that the most rapid gains in per capita income are not necessarily found among the fastest-growing places.

Rates of Change in Employment

Group rates of growth in employment for the entire 1974–97 period (see table 1.6) show that resort/retirement places are clearly the fastest growing, followed by government/service metros. The slowest growing were the manufacturing-oriented places: the functional nodal, manufacturing/service, and manufacturing groups. The nodal, government/service, and government/military places tended to fall in a middle position.

When the growth experiences of the two subperiods (1974–90 and 1990–97) are compared for each type/size metro group (table 1.7), we observe certain continuities, but also several marked changes. In general, the resort/retirement groups continued to be among the fastest growing during the 1990s, and the manufacturing-oriented groups (functional nodal, manufacturing service, and manufacturing), the slowest. But there were important changes, the most dramatic being among the *small nodal* metros (with less than 250,000 population). This group, which had been ranked ninth, rose to first place.

Table 1.7 also presents for each type/size group distributions of metros among three growth categories: high, medium, and low. These categories were based on a ranking of all metros according to their growth rates during the period 1974–90, and again during the period 1990–97.[8] The distributions provide a clearer picture of the growth experience than does a single rate of employment growth.

In both periods, growth rates vary among metros within every type/size group (note, however, that in each group there are places ranked in each growth category). Further, changes in overall growth rates from the first to the second period are generally consistent with changes in the distribution of places among the high, medium, and low categories.

The distributions are particularly interesting in what they tell about the difference in the growth experience among the nodal groups. During the 1990s, fewer places among the two larger nodal groups were characterized by relatively high growth rates than had been the case in the preceding period. But among smaller nodal groups, especially those with less than 250,000 population, the distribution of rankings was more favorable during the 1990s.

TABLE 1.6

Rates of Growth in Employment, Earnings per Worker, Earnings per Capita, and
Income per Capita, by Type/Size of Metro Group, 1974–97

Type/Size Group	Rate of Growth[a,b]							
	Employment		Earnings per Worker		Earnings per Capita		Income per Capita	
Nodal								
> 2 Million	1.76	(10)	0.28	(1)	1.21	(2–3)	1.51	(4)
1–2 Million	2.08	(7)	0.07	(3)	1.21	(2–3)	1.53	(2–3)
250,000–1 Million	2.03	(8)	0.14	(2)	1.30	(1)	1.71	(1)
< 250,000	2.33	(6)	−0.49	(14)	0.59	(13)	1.29	(9)
Functional Nodal[c]								
> 250,000	1.50	(13)	−0.08	(7)	1.00	(4)	1.45	(5)
Manufacturing/Service								
> 250,000	1.37	(14)	−0.04	(5)	0.86	(7)	1.38	(7)
< 250,000	1.64	(11)	−0.41	(12)	0.68	(11)	1.28	(10)
Manufacturing[d]								
> 250,000	1.42	(12)	−0.22	(9)	0.65	(12)	1.21	(13)
Government/Service								
> 250,000	2.68	(3)	−0.12	(8)	0.90	(6)	1.31	(8)
< 250,000	2.62	(4)	−0.25	(11)	0.94	(5)	1.42	(6)
Government/Military								
> 250,000	2.56	(5)	0.00	(4)	0.73	(9–10)	1.24	(11–12)
< 250,000	1.88	(9)	−0.47	(13)	0.1	(14)	0.91	(14)
Resort/Retirement								
> 250,000	4.01	(1)	−0.06	(6)	0.85	(8)	1.24	(11–12)
< 250,000	3.78	(2)	−0.24	(10)	0.73	(9–10)	1.53	(2–3)

Notes: a. Ranks are shown in parentheses.

b. Deflated by the U.S. consumer price index.

c.,d. Because of the small number of metros with populations of less than 250,000 classified as functional nodal (five metros) and manufacturing (five metros), measures for these size-type groups are not shown in the tables throughout this book. See page 30.

Source: U.S. Bureau of Economic Analysis.

Among the functional nodal and manufacturing groups, there was little difference in distributions from the first period to the last. For the manufacturing/service groups, however, this was not the case: Among the larger metros (with populations of 250,000 or more), there was a sharp drop in the number of metros ranked high; among the smaller (with populations of less than 250,000), there was a significant increase.

The government/service and government/military distributions did not change greatly from the 1974–90 period to the 1990s, although in both types of metro the smaller group tended to fare better. In both size groups of resort/retirement metros, there was a sharp decline in highly ranked places, although during the 1990s overall growth rates for both of these groups remained at a relatively high level.

TABLE 1.7

Rates of Growth in Employment and Distribution of Growth Rates, by Type/Size Metro Group, 1974–90 and 1990–97

Type/Size Group	Rate of Growth, 1974–90					Rate of Growth, 1990–97				
	Average	Rank	Distribution[a]			Average	Rank	Distribution[a]		
			H	M	L			H	M	L
Nodal										
> 2 Million	2.05	7	37.5	31.2	31.2	1.10	13	25.0	6.2	68.8
1–2 Million	2.18	6	33.3	38.9	27.8	1.86	8	27.8	33.3	38.9
250,000–1 Million	2.04	8	22.7	59.1	18.2	1.99	5	36.4	45.4	18.2
< 250,000	2.04	9	31.2	37.5	31.2	3.00	1	56.2	37.5	6.2
Functional Nodal										
> 250,000	1.61	11	5.9	35.3	58.8	1.24	12	5.9	47.1	47.1
Manufacturing/Service										
> 250,000	1.59	12	33.3	8.3	58.3	0.86	14	8.3	33.3	58.3
< 250,000	1.59	13	9.1	31.8	59.1	1.76	9	22.7	31.8	45.4
Manufacturing										
> 250,000	1.32	14	4.6	31.8	63.6	1.63	11	18.2	18.2	63.6
Government/Service										
> 250,000	3.01	3	51.5	42.4	6.1	1.94	6	42.4	30.3	27.3
< 250,000	2.76	5	55.2	31.0	13.8	2.30	4	55.2	31.0	13.8
Government/Military										
> 250,000	2.93	4	31.2	50.0	18.8	1.72	10	31.2	31.2	37.5
< 250,000	1.87	10	14.3	33.3	52.4	1.90	7	14.3	57.1	28.6
Resort/Retirement										
> 250,000	4.50	1	100.0	0.0	0.0	2.74	2	46.2	30.8	23.1
< 250,000	4.34	2	91.7	0.0	8.3	2.68	3	58.3	33.3	8.3
United States	2.08	—	—	—	—	1.68	—	—	—	—

Note: a. "H" indicates the percentage of metros in the group within the top third of the array of rankings of all metros. "M" indicates the percentage of the group within the middle third. "L" indicates the percentage of the group within the lowest third.

Source: U.S. Bureau of Economic Analysis.

Rates of Change in Earnings per Worker

All groups of metros (except the nodal metros with more than 250,000 population) showed declines or no change in earnings per worker, although there were significant differences in rates of change among many of the groups (see table 1.6).[9] When rankings of groups for rates of change in earnings are compared with those for employment growth, we observe marked differences. Of special note are the larger nodal metros (the three groups with populations of 250,000 or more). These groups ranked near the top (first, third, and second) in rate of change in earnings, but roughly in the middle (tenth, seventh, and eighth) in employment growth. The two resort/retirement groups, conversely, showed the highest rankings in employment growth but were in the middle range of rates of change in earnings per worker.

Rates of Change in Earnings per Capita

Rates of change in earnings per capita were everywhere sharply higher than rates of change in earnings per worker (see table 1.6), reflecting principally the impact of the entry of the over-sized baby boom generation into the workforce and the sharply increased employment of women, generally, resulting in a larger proportion of the populace in the workforce (see table 1.6). In most groups of metros, rankings were similar to those for rates of change in earnings per worker.

Rates of Change in Income per Capita

Rates of change in income per capita (see table 1.6) were everywhere higher than in earnings per capita, reflecting the rapidly increasing importance of non-earned income (i.e., TP and DIR), which is discussed below. When growth rates for income per capita were compared with those for earnings per capita, the larger nodal groups continued to rank high, with the average rate of increase in income per capita among the very large nodal places ranking them in fourth place.

The Increased Importance of Non-Earned Income

Little attention has been paid by students of metropolitan economies to the role played by non-earned income. Yet dividends, interest, and rent payments, along with transfer payments (principally Social Security, Medicare, Medicaid, and welfare), provide major flows of income—which, like earnings, may be spent in the local marketplace and which, to varying degrees, are sources of taxable income for local governments. Thus non-earned income, like earned income, contributes to aggregate demand and indirectly to the demand for labor in the metropolitan economy.

Table 1.8 shows that non-earned income contributes significantly to total income everywhere but plays a much more important role in some metropolitan economies than in others. Further, non-earned income increased in importance everywhere from 1974 to 1997. In 1997,

TABLE 1.8
Earnings; Transfer Payments (TP); and Dividends, Interest, and Rent (DIR) Payments
as Shares (Percentage) of Total Personal Income;
by Type and Size of Metro Group, 1974 and 1997

Type/Size Group		1974			1997		
		Earnings	TP	DIR	Earnings	TP	DIR
Nodal	> 2 Million	73.03	12.28	14.69	68.36	14.49	17.15
Nodal	1–2 Million	74.51	10.58	14.91	69.29	13.15	17.56
Nodal	250,000–1 Million	75.50	11.31	13.19	68.81	14.65	16.54
Nodal	< 250,000	77.86	11.43	13.51	66.27	16.52	17.21
Functional Nodal	> 250,000	76.25	11.09	12.66	68.90	14.64	16.46
Manufacturing/Service	> 250,000	73.02	13.73	13.25	64.74	18.86	16.40
Manufacturing/Service	< 250,000	74.38	13.41	12.21	64.79	18.99	16.22
Manufacturing	> 250,000	77.06	11.21	11.73	67.84	16.44	15.72
Government/Service	> 250,000	74.52	12.59	12.89	67.81	15.60	16.59
Government/Service	< 250,000	73.78	12.41	13.81	66.22	15.98	17.80
Government/Military	> 250,000	73.56	13.93	12.52	65.53	18.29	16.18
Government/Military	< 250,000	75.82	13.37	10.81	63.03	22.14	14.83
Resort/Retirement	> 250,000	65.08	14.82	20.10	59.64	17.63	22.74
Resort/Retirement	< 250,000	65.83	14.81	19.36	54.85	18.67	26.49
United States		73.63	12.53	13.85	66.38	16.40	17.22

Source: U.S. Bureau of Economic Analysis.

TP ranged from 13 to 22 percent of total personal income; DIR, from just under 15 to more than 26 percent.

Clearly, the size and exact nature of non-earned income payments influence the metropolitan economy. Not only do they contribute to aggregate demand; they also influence the mix of local-sector demand. For example, high proportions of TP and DIR often indicate a relatively high proportion of retired persons heavily dependent on pensions, investment income, or both. Such persons are likely to demand a different array of goods and services than would a younger, less affluent working-age segment of the population.

Moreover, DIR and certain types of TP (especially Social Security benefits and Medicare) are highly portable. Thus the growth processes of the economies of resort/retirement places may differ sharply from other types of metro economies, in that the in-migration of new residents and the income they carry with them may stimulate growth in demand for types of goods and services and for labor quite different from those of other metro economies in which industrial growth is the primary stimulant of increases in employment.

The Threefold Transformation

The preceding sections suggest not only that there have been major changes within the metropolitan system but that these changes may be regarded as a threefold transformation.

First, there has been a transformation in employment. The sharply changing industrial composition of employment brought about by the declining importance of goods production and the increasing importance of certain services has led to a transformation in the composition of employment within the U.S. job market.

Second, there has been a transformation in earnings. The level of average earnings (for combined industries) has changed differentially among groups of metros, which meant that some groups fared better than others during the 1974–97 period. We shall find in chapter 5 that earnings levels per worker in the various industrial categories have changed differentially, and that these changes have also played an important role in this transformation of earnings.

Third, there has been a transformation in the nature and sources of total income. Clearly, increases in non-earned income—TP and DIR—have affected the various metros to different degrees. Accordingly, these increases have contributed to changes in the demand for human and nonhuman resources within metros, and thus to the ability of metros to gain or to retain economic vitality.

Plan of the Study

In brief, the plan of this study is to examine the principal characteristics of the several type/size groups of metros and to analyze the changes that have affected these metros as part of the three transformations. Chapter 2 presents the results of a classification procedure based on 1990 employment data and examines the evidence for specialization among and within the several metro groups. Chapter 3 sketches relevant theory on the nature of metropolitan growth.

Returning to the empirical level, chapter 4 examines the impact that the shift from goods to services has had on employment, and in turn on metros' export sectors and their prospects for growth and vitality. Chapter 5 treats the transformation in both earnings and the composition of income. Levels of industry earnings per worker among the various type/size metro groups are compared, followed by an analysis of the growth rates of the three major income types and of the implications of these observed trends. A final section highlights characteristic levels and rates of growth of earnings, TP, DIR, and total income among the several type/size groups. Chapter 6 summarizes the principal findings of the study.

Notes

1. T. J. Noyelle and T. M. Stanback, Jr., *The economic transformation of American cities* (Totowa, NJ: Rowman and Allanheld, 1983). A still earlier, shorter study of the metropolitan economy is T. M. Stanback, Jr., and R. V. Knight, *The metropolitan economy* (New York, NY: Columbia University Press, 1970).

2. In the revised format, transportation, communications, and utilities has been broken down into two subcategories: (1) transportation and (2) communications/utilities; finance, insurance, and real estate into three subgroups: (1) banking, (2) insurance carriers, and (3) FIRE brokers and agents; nonprofit services into three subgroups: (1) health services, (2) educational services, and (3) social services/organizations; and government into three subgroups: (1) federal, (2) military, and (3) state and local. Business/professional services is similar to the earlier classification "corporate services" but does not include membership organizations (Standard Industrial Classification [SIC] 86), museums and the like (SIC 84), and social services (SIC 86), which appear as the subcategory social services/organizations. The remaining categories (mining, construction, retail, wholesale, and administration and auxiliary) are essentially the same as were utilized in the earlier study.

3. Job increases were determined for the United States by calculating the *net* change in employment for each of the industrial categories *in which there was an employment increase*. Total job increases were then distributed.

4. The terms "metropolitan economies" and "metros" are used interchangeably throughout this study.

5. The sense in which location quotients may be regarded as evidence of "specialization" is discussed at the beginning of chapter 2.

6. It is important to recognize that, where gains occur in a given broadly defined service category, the specific services experiencing growth may vary across type/size groups of metros. For example: Rapid, ubiquitous growth of employment in business/professional services could be expected to be limited in smaller metros to consumer-oriented and small-business services. In larger, diversified service centers, however, the list is likely to include not only these lower-level consumer and small-business services but also a variety of sophisticated, high-value-added services.

7. The method of classification is discussed in chapter 2 and appendix A.

8. Rates of change in employment in individual metros were distributed among three categories: high, medium, and low. In defining these categories, *all* metros were ranked from highest to lowest, and the rankings were broken into three equal groups: highest (top third), middle (middle third), and lowest (bottom third). The numbers of metros ranked within the highest, middle, and lowest growth categories were then determined for each type/size group of metros, and the results were distributed as percentages.

9. In all deflations of earnings and income, the U.S. consumer price index (CPI) was used as a deflator.

2

The Industrial Specialization
of Metropolitan Economies

An important preliminary task for analyzing changes within the U.S. urban system is to classify metropolitan areas. This chapter sets forth the result of the classification process as it was applied to metros in 1990 and examines the roles and relative importance of the various types of places within the overall metro system. The final section of the chapter presents evidence of the dominant role played by large, diversified service centers (i.e., large nodal metros) in providing corporate services, along with brief profiles of the economies of the six metros that are the major providers of these services.

Classification of Metropolitan Areas

The classification procedure was essentially the same as that in *The Economic Transformation of American Cities*: Statistical clustering was used to group all metropolitan areas in the continental United States on the basis of similarities in their industrial composition of employment, as measured by location quotients calculated with 1990 data.[1]

The classification analysis resulted in three broad groupings, with seven categories or types:[2]

Grouping and type	Number of metros
Diversified service centers (nodal metros)	88
Production centers	
Functional nodal	22
Manufacturing/service	56
Manufacturing	27
Specialized service centers	
Government/service	62
Government/military	37
Resort/retirement	25
Total	317

These categories were further broken down into population size groups (based on 1990 population). Nodal metros were divided into four population groups: 2 million and more, 1 million to 2 million, 250,000 to 1 million, and less than 250,000. The remaining categories were broken down into only two size groups: 250,000 or more, and less than 250,000.[3] Table 2.1 presents a list of metros in each type/size group. This breakdown recognizes the importance of size as a variable affecting the nature and extent of specialization, even though certain patterns of specialization remain within each classification, regardless of size.

Employment Location Quotients as Measures of Industrial Specialization

Urban economists and geographers frequently use location quotients to identify industries that are part of the export economic base of a city or region. Their logic is straightforward. It is assumed that the nation as a whole is self-sufficient, and that the national share of employment accounted for by each industry accordingly may be regarded as a norm (i.e., the U.S. LQ for each industry is 1.00).[4] LQs can then be calculated for each industrial category in each city or region by expressing the share of employment relative to the national norm.

Taken literally, an LQ greater than 1.00 could be interpreted as indicating that the industry produces more than is necessary for its needs and consequently is part of the city's or region's export sector. Similarly, an LQ of less than 1.00 would indicate some importing.

Such a literal interpretation, however, is not warranted—for two reasons. First, the national economy is not self-sufficient, and the U.S. industrial structure is not an ideal norm. Second and more important, the economic systems of metropolitan and nonmetropolitan areas are highly interdependent: An LQ of 1.00 does *not* indicate that a metropolitan economy is self-sufficient in the production of the goods and services within that industrial category. Quite the contrary, there may be both lively importing and exporting of goods or services within an industry in a given place. Similarly, an LQ of less than 1.00 need not indicate that there are no firms exporting goods or services. This is especially true in manufacturing, where economic production typically involves reaching out to a market broader than the given metropolitan area in which a plant is based. The LQ for the manufacturing sector may be quite low, and yet it likely includes firms producing and shipping goods to outside markets.

Yet in spite of these limitations, employment LQs provide an important tool for analyzing metropolitan industrial composition and patterns of development. These LQs measure the extent to which a metro's employment in an industrial category is over- or underrepresented relative to the national economy as a whole. Although it does not pinpoint individual-firm specialization, it does indicate the industrial categories in which the metropolitan economy is or is not specializing, in the sense that it is allocating abnormally large or small shares of its human resources.

TABLE 2.1
U.S. Metropolitan Areas Classified by Type and Size, 1990, with 1990 Population (in thousands)

Nodal > 2 Million	Population	Nodal 250,000–1 Million (cont'd.)	Population
Los Angeles–Long Beach, CA	8,741.4	Omaha, NE–IA	614.3
New York, NY	8,538.5	Knoxville, TN	602.0
Chicago, IL	6,061.9	Harrisburg–Lebanon–Carlisle, PA	584.8
Philadelphia, PA–NJ	4,843.2	Lake County, IL	509.4
Boston–Lawrence–Salem–Lowell, MA	3,787.6	Mobile, AL	473.9
Houston, TX	3,267.1	Jackson, MS	393.8
Atlanta, GA	2,783.0	Des Moines, IA	388.6
Nassau–Suffolk, NY	2,614.1	Fort Wayne, IN	361.2
Dallas, TX	2,508.6	Spokane, WA	356.4
Saint Louis, MO–IL	2,436.3	Portsmouth–Dover–Rochester, NH	347.6
Minneapolis–Saint Paul, MN–WI	2,429.5	Manchester–Nashua, NH	334.7
Anaheim–Santa Ana, CA	2,367.7	Charleston, WV	252.1
Baltimore, MD	2,363.1		
Phoenix, AZ	2,094.9	**Nodal < 250,000**	
Pittsburgh, PA	2,068.0	South Bend, IN	245.9
Oakland, CA	2,052.8	Portland, ME	241.0
		Odessa–Midland, TX	226.1
Nodal 1–2 Million		Roanoke, VA	224.9
Seattle, WA	1,915.3	Lubbock, TX	221.3
Miami–Hialeah, FL	1,904.6	Lafayette, LA*	209.2
Newark, NJ	1,834.8	Boise City, ID*	207.5
Cleveland, OH	1,834.6	Green Bay, WI	192.5
Denver, CO	1,615.9	Ocala, FL	188.5
San Francisco, CA	1,595.7	Amarillo, TX	186.7
Kansas City, MO–KS	1,553.5	Yakima, WA	185.6
Cincinnati, OH–KY–IN	1,445.6	Houma, LA	184.1
Milwaukee, WI	1,422.0	Lake Charles, LA	168.8
Columbus, OH	1,364.1	Cedar Rapids, IA	167.5
Fort Worth–Arlington, TX	1,307.8	Wheeling, WV–OH	161.2
Bergen–Passaic, NJ	1,284.6	Fargo–Moorhead, ND–MN	152.6
New Orleans, LA	1,249.8	Tyler, TX	150.0
Indianapolis, IN	1,239.9	Saint Cloud, MN	147.3
Portland, OR	1,214.1	Medford–Ashland, OR	143.4
Charlotte–Gastonia–Rock Hill, NC–SC	1,144.9	Monroe, LA	142.7
Salt Lake City–Ogden, UT	1,061.1	Sioux Falls, SD	138.5
Middlesex–Somerset–Hunterdon, NJ	1,012.2	Yolo, CA	138.4
		Laredo, TX	130.2
Nodal 250,000–1 Million		Kenosha, WI	126.9
Memphis, TN–AR–MS	976.5	Bloomington–Normal, IL	126.6
Nashville, TN	973.5	La Crosse, WI–MN	115.5
Buffalo, NY	972.8	Sioux City, IA–NE	114.5
Louisville, KY–IN	950.4	Billings, MT	113.7
Birmingham, AL	905.0	Kankakee, IL	96.4
Jacksonville, FL	889.6	Victoria, TX	74.2
Richmond–Petersburg, VA	855.6	Casper, WY	62.6
Bridgeport–Stamford–Norwalk, CT	829.9	Enid, OK	57.7
Tulsa, OK	707.8		
Syracuse, NY	660.0		

TABLE 2.1 (continued)
U.S. Metropolitan Areas Classified by Type and Size, 1990, with 1990 Population (in thousands)

Functional Nodal >250,000	Population	Manufacturing/Service < 250,000 (cont'd.)	Population
Detroit, MI	4,372.0	Jackson, MI	148.7
San Jose, CA	1,480.4	Richland–Kennewick–Pasco, WA	148.5
Hartford–New Britain–Middletown, CT	1,121.0	Terre Haute, IN	147.9
Rochester, NY	1,002.1	Bangor, ME	145.7
Dayton–Springfield, OH	948.5	Steubenville–Weirton, OH–WV	144.5
Greensboro–Winston-Salem–High Point, NC	933.5	Jamestown, NY	142.6
Worcester–Fitchburg–Leominster, MA	706.4	Pittsfield, MA	140.5
Allentown–Bethlehem–Easton, PA	681.4	Janesville–Beloit, WI	139.1
Akron, OH	656.1	Vineland–Millville–Bridgeton, NJ	137.9
Greenville–Spartanburg, SC	634.9	Eau Claire, WI	136.6
Wilmington, DE–NJ–MD	572.5	Joplin, MO	134.2
Jersey City, NJ	556.4	Florence, AL	131.9
Wichita, KS	482.4	Greeley, CO	131.6
Kalamazoo–Battle Creek, MI*	429.5	Decatur, AL	130.9
Saginaw–Bay City–Midland, MI	398.9	Altoona, PA	130.8
Peoria, IL	339.7	Waterloo–Cedar Falls, IA	124.2
Appleton–Oshkosh–Neenah, WI	312.4	Sharon, PA	121.5
		Hagerstown, MD	120.4
Functional Nodal < 250,000		Muncie, IN	120.0
Fayetteville–Springdale–Rogers, AR	208.0	Williamsport, PA	118.4
Racine, WI	174.1	Glens Falls, NY	117.8
Rocky Mount, NC	132.4	Wausau, WI	114.6
Decatur, IL	118.2	Florence, SC	114.0
Sheboygan, WI	103.3	Lewiston–Auburn, ME	104.8
		Gadsden, AL	100.0
Manufacturing/Service > 250,000		Saint Joseph, MO	97.9
Providence–Pawtucket–Woonsocket, RI	913.4	Elmira, NY	95.2
New Haven–Waterbury–Meriden, CT	802.6	Sherman–Denison, TX	94.7
Scranton–Wilkes-Barre, PA	732.3	Owensboro, KY	86.9
Toledo, OH	613.4	Dubuque, IA	86.3
Springfield, MA	603.1	Pine Bluff, AR	85.8
Augusta, GA–SC	394.1	Jackson, TN*	78.0
Beaumont–Port Arthur, TX	362.5		
Modesto, CA	360.9	**Manufacturing > 250,000**	
Ann Arbor, MI	280.7	Grand Rapids, MI	679.8
Lorain–Elyria, OH	271.2	Gary–Hammond, IN	605.4
Springfield, MO*	264.3	New Bedford–Fall River–Attleboro, MA	506.4
Poughkeepsie, NY	258.8	Youngstown–Warren, OH	495.6
		Johnson City–Kingsport–Bristol, TN	436.5
Manufacturing/Service < 250,000		Chattanooga, TN–GA	431.5
Johnstown, PA	242.9	Flint, MI	430.6
Boulder–Longmont, CO	223.3	Lancaster, PA	417.1
Longview–Marshall, TX	193.6	York, PA	414.1
Lynchburg, VA	193.3	Canton, OH	394.5
Brazoria, TX	190.8	Joliet, IL	386.0
Asheville, NC	190.6	Aurora–Elgin, IL	352.9
Waco, TX	187.8	Davenport–Rock Island–Moline, IA–IL	352.5
Burlington, VT	175.1	Reading, PA	334.0
Fort Smith, AR–OK	174.8	Huntington–Ashland, WV–KY–OH	314.2
Lafayette, IN	160.6	Hamilton–Middletown, OH	288.4
Lima, OH	154.1	Hickory–Morganton, NC*	292.4
Parkersburg–Marietta, WV–OH	149.8	Rockford, IL	282.8

TABLE 2.1 (continued)
U.S. Metropolitan Areas Classified by Type and Size, 1990, with 1990 Population (in thousands)

Manufacturing > 250,000 (cont'd.)	Population	Government/Service < 250,000	Population
Evansville, IN–KY	278.4	Duluth–Superior, MN–WI	240.9
Erie, PA	276.1	Tallahassee, FL	229.1
Binghamton, NY	265.0	Santa Cruz–Watsonville, CA	226.5
New London–Norwich, CT	254.9	Galveston–Texas City, TX	216.5
		San Luis Obispo–Atascad.–Pasadena, CA	212.6
Manufacturing < 250,000		Lincoln, NE	211.5
Mansfield, OH	174.4	Springfield, IL	189.1
Benton Harbor, MI	161.0	Fort Collins–Loveland, CO	183.5
Elkhart–Goshen, IN	154.3	Gainesville, FL	178.7
Danville, VA	110.6	Champaign–Urbana, IL	172.5
Kokomo, IN	97.5	Topeka, KS	160.6
		Olympia, WA	156.4
Government/Service > 250,000		Tuscaloosa, AL	149.1
Washington, DC–MD–VA	3,878.7	Las Cruces, NM	134.5
Sacramento, CA	1,446.0	Dothan, AL	130.5
Monmouth–Ocean, NJ	978.5	Charlottesville, VA	129.9
Oklahoma City, OK	957.0	Athens, GA	125.0
Albany–Schenectady–Troy, NY	872.5	Pueblo, CO	123.3
Austin, TX	765.4	State College, PA	122.9
Raleigh–Durham, NC	720.9	Bryan–College Station, TX	121.0
Tucson, AZ	661.0	Santa Fe, NM	114.8
Oxnard–Ventura, CA	656.3	Albany, GA	113.0
Fresno, CA	654.0	Columbia, MO	111.6
Bakersfield, CA	532.9	Bloomington, IN	107.9
Baton Rouge, LA	530.2	Greenville, NC	106.3
Little Rock–North Little Rock, AR	510.4	Iowa City, IA	94.5
Albuquerque, NM	475.8	Bismarck, ND	84.3
Stockton, CA	470.4	Lawrence, KS	80.6
Columbia, SC	449.5	Cheyenne, WY	72.9
Lansing–East Lansing, MI	430.2		
Santa Rosa–Petaluma, CA	379.8	**Government/Military > 250,000**	
McAllen–Edinburg–Mission, TX	375.9	San Diego, CA	2,439.6
Madison, WI	362.4	Norfolk–Virginia B.–Newport News, VA	1,378.6
Corpus Christi, TX	349.1	San Antonio, TX	1,283.8
Lexington–Fayette, KY	344.0	El Paso, TX	582.0
Shreveport, LA	337.0	Tacoma, WA	570.5
Trenton, NJ	324.9	Charleston, SC	500.6
Utica–Rome, NY	317.7	Vallejo–Fairfield–Napa, CA	441.0
Visalia–Tulare–Porterville, CA	306.7	Colorado Springs, CO	391.9
Orange County, NY	304.0	Salinas–Seaside–Monterey, CA	351.2
Montgomery, AL	292.1	Pensacola, FL	339.1
Eugene–Springfield, OR	278.0	Biloxi-Gulfport–Pascagoula, MS	312.4
Salem, OR	272.6	Huntsville, AL*	293.0
Provo–Orem, UT	260.3	Macon–Warner Robins, GA	280.5
Savannah, GA*	258.1	Fayetteville, NC	273.0
Brownsville–Harlingen, TX	256.8	Columbus, GA–AL*	260.9
		Killeen–Temple, TX	251.7

TABLE 2.1 (continued)
U.S. Metropolitan Areas Classified by Type and Size, 1990, with 1990 Population (in thousands)

Government/Military < 250,000	Population	Resort/Retirement < 250,000	Population
Bremerton, WA	183.9	Reno, NV	243.4
Merced, CA	175.1	Fort Pierce–Port Saint Lucie, FL	241.6
Clarksville–Hopkinsville, TN–KY	167.4	Barnstable–Yarmouth, MA	184.3
Jacksonville, NC	147.2	Chico–Paradise, CA	178.9
Fort Walton Beach, FL	141.0	Naples, FL	145.8
Alexandria, LA	132.5	Redding, CA	144.3
Wichita Falls, TX	130.1	Myrtle Beach, SC	141.0
Panama City, FL	124.8	Bellingham, WA	124.4
Yuba City, CA	120.9	Wilmington, NC	119.0
Texarkana, TX–Texarkana, AR	119.7	Punta Gorda, FL	106.0
Abilene, TX	119.6	Rochester, MN	105.1
Anniston, AL	116.7	Cumberland, MD–WV	101.8
Lawton, OK	111.9		
Dover, DE	109.7	**Unclassified**	
Goldsboro, NC	103.9	Honolulu, HI*	828.5
Grand Forks, ND–MN	103.4	Anchorage, AK*	227.6
Yuma, AZ	103.4		
Sumter, SC	101.5		
San Angelo, TX	97.5		
Rapid City, SD	80.3		
Great Falls, MT	77.9		

Resort/Retirement > 250,000

Riverside–San Bernardino, CA	2,488.4
Tampa–St. Petersburg–Clearwater, FL	2,026.9
Ft. Lauderdale–Hollywood–Pompano B., FL	1,231.2
Orlando, FL	1,038.2
West Palm Beach–Boca Raton, FL	837.8
Las Vegas, NV	698.4
Lakeland–Winter Haven, FL	397.3
Melbourne–Titusville–Palm Bay, FL	388.3
Santa Barbara–Santa Maria–Lompoc, CA	364.6
Daytona Beach, FL	359.9
Fort Myers–Cape Coral, FL	323.1
Atlantic City, NJ	316.7
Sarasota, FL	271.0

Note: The ten metros marked with an asterisk (*) were not included in the various analyses in this and the following chapters.

Source: U.S. Department of Commerce, U.S. Bureau of the Census.

This use of LQs to define economic specialization is grounded in trade theory and the concept of comparative advantage. Under free-market conditions, metropolitan economies will tend to develop so as to maximize their competitive (comparative) advantage in trade, and resources will move into the industries that produce the goods or services best suited to this maximizing. Under such conditions, metros will become specialized in certain types of activities, and this specialization will be manifest in the disproportionate share of resources allocated to these activities.

To be sure, the measure used in this study—the employment location quotient—informs us of the allocation of only one of the factors of production: labor. Employment is an imperfect proxy for value added (which is the preferred measure), because the mix of labor, capital, and land in a given industrial category may vary from firm to firm and place to place (especially in light of the fairly broad range of activities included within each category). Moreover, average levels of skills, experience, and training may also vary.[5] But there are at least two excellent reasons to use employment measures. First, labor is the largest factor input in metropolitan economies, and interest centers on the location and trends of growth of employment and population. Second, employment data are the only data available at the county level at a quite detailed industrial breakdown (earnings data are also available, but with less satisfactory coverage).

The position taken here is that employment LQs provide a highly useful—though imprecise—measure of the extent to which labor is allocated to each of the several industrial categories within each metro, and that those categories with relatively high LQs may be regarded as specialized and as part of the metropolitan economy's export sector. In making use of LQs, I have tried to avoid arbitrary judgments as to the exact LQ levels that determine specialization, candidacy for export-base status, and so on.

To measure the extent of specialization in the following sections, I use not only LQs computed for each metro group (table 2.2) but also analyze LQ rankings for individual metros (tables 2.3 and 2.4). In preparing the measures presented in tables 2.3 and 2.4, the procedure was to rank for each industrial category the LQs of all metros within the metropolitan system of the continental United States, and then to calculate for each type/size metro group the percentage of places that fall within each quintile of the entire array for each industrial category. This measure supplements the type/size group LQs (which are actually group averages weighted by employment) by indicating the percentage of individual metros within each group that have a relatively high level of specialization (i.e., that rank within the top two quintiles).

Industrial Characteristics of Metro Groups, 1997

Nodal Metros

The larger-size nodal metro groups are specialized in providing a variety of services, especially intermediate services provided to large and small businesses and the services provided to corporations by headquarters and other administrative offices (administration/auxiliary [A/A]). For the *group with 2 million or more population* (e.g., Atlanta, Chicago, Los Angeles, New York, and Phoenix),[6] the group LQs for FIRE, business/professional services, and A/A are 1.34, 1.35, and 1.36, respectively. The LQ for the combined high-tech goods and services classifications (discussed below) is also quite high, 1.37, with 9 of these 16 places ranked in the top quintile

TABLE 2.2
Location Quotients by Type/Size Metro Group, 1997

Industrial Category	N_1	N_2	N_3	N_4	FN_1	MS_1	MS_2	Mfg_1	GS_1	GS_2	GM_1	GM_2	RR_1	RR_2
Construction	0.91	1.02	1.06	1.07	0.95	0.86	1.04	1.07	1.10	1.04	1.08	0.92	1.31	1.44
Manufacturing	0.85	0.93	0.90	0.86	1.45	1.22	1.39	1.55	0.61	0.62	0.63	0.66	0.54	0.55
Transportation, Communications, and Utilities	1.17	1.34	1.18	1.04	0.87	0.77	0.83	0.82	0.84	0.70	0.78	0.60	0.92	0.83
Transportation	1.21	1.40	1.14	1.08	0.90	0.73	0.81	0.82	0.73	0.62	0.74	0.54	0.94	0.83
Communications and Utilities	1.10	1.19	1.05	1.03	0.85	0.85	0.92	0.85	1.07	0.87	0.88	0.75	0.92	0.90
Wholesale Trade	1.23	1.28	1.14	1.12	1.06	0.76	0.81	0.99	0.81	0.58	0.76	0.60	0.90	0.74
Retail Trade	0.89	0.97	1.03	1.16	0.96	1.03	1.10	1.09	0.98	1.08	0.99	1.07	1.15	1.33
Finance, Insurance, and Real Estate (FIRE)	1.34	1.24	1.21	0.98	1.01	0.78	0.67	0.69	0.92	0.76	0.81	0.59	0.97	0.81
Banking/Credit Agencies	1.20	1.18	1.20	0.97	0.97	0.78	0.85	0.82	0.83	0.73	0.84	0.76	0.91	0.81
Insurance Carriers	1.23	1.42	1.67	1.52	1.37	1.12	0.67	0.72	1.11	0.91	0.75	0.32	0.64	0.29
FIRE Agents and Brokers	1.51	1.18	1.00	0.74	0.85	0.64	0.55	0.57	0.91	0.71	0.81	0.59	1.21	1.10
Business/Professional Services	1.35	1.17	1.01	0.77	1.10	0.76	0.67	0.71	1.22	0.70	0.95	0.57	1.27	0.83
Nonprofit Services	1.04	0.93	1.03	1.10	0.98	1.28	1.10	1.01	1.01	1.05	0.91	0.94	0.92	1.10
Health Services	0.99	0.93	1.03	1.13	0.97	1.30	1.13	1.04	0.93	1.12	0.94	1.06	1.00	1.28
Educational Services	1.41	0.87	0.93	0.93	1.08	1.68	1.00	0.80	1.10	0.62	0.72	0.40	0.57	0.40
Social Services/Organizations	0.99	0.96	1.08	1.10	0.93	1.03	1.08	1.03	1.17	1.09	0.94	0.92	0.87	0.98
Consumer Services	1.05	0.97	0.90	0.98	0.78	0.78	0.81	0.96	0.89	0.85	1.05	0.83	2.09	1.95
Government/Services														
Federal	0.83	0.87	0.92	0.66	0.64	0.79	0.61	0.58	2.31	0.89	2.10	2.47	0.67	0.56
Military	0.44	0.46	0.99	0.60	0.42	0.68	0.52	0.56	1.18	0.68	5.85	8.24	0.73	0.46
State and Local	0.82	0.83	0.87	1.00	0.79	1.10	1.05	0.82	1.24	1.97	0.99	1.07	0.88	0.98
Administration/Auxiliary	1.36	1.48	1.34	0.80	1.77	0.83	0.48	0.64	0.79	0.36	0.51	0.24	0.78	0.30

Note: For definitions of type/size group codes, see note 3 to chapter 2.
Source: *County Business Patterns.*

TABLE 2.3

Percentage of Metros with Location Quotients Ranked in Top Two Quintiles, by Industrial Category for Each Type/Size Metro Group, 1997

Industrial Category	N_1	N_2	N_3	N_4	FN_1	MS_1	MS_2	Mfg_1	GS_1	GS_2	GM_1	GM_2	RR_1	RR_2
Construction	50.0	44.5	45.5	40.0	37.5	27.3	30.2	38.1	43.8	34.5	53.8	23.8	76.9	75.0
Manufacturing	25.0	38.9	27.3	26.7	81.2	72.7	90.7	95.2	6.2	13.8	0.0	14.3	0.0	0.0
Transportation, Communications, and Utilities	75.0	88.9	72.7	56.7	37.5	27.3	37.2	33.3	28.1	17.2	15.4	9.5	38.5	33.3
Transportation	93.8	94.4	72.7	56.7	31.2	27.3	25.6	42.9	28.1	10.3	23.1	4.8	46.2	33.3
Communications and Utilities	50.0	61.1	36.4	56.7	31.2	27.3	39.5	38.1	43.8	34.5	38.5	23.8	30.8	33.3
Wholesale Trade	87.5	88.9	90.9	70.0	56.2	0.0	23.3	47.6	34.4	3.4	7.7	14.3	30.8	16.7
Retail Trade	0.0	11.1	18.2	73.0	18.8	36.4	51.2	47.6	34.4	41.4	23.1	42.9	69.2	83.3
Finance, Insurance, and Real Estate (FIRE)	100.0	94.4	90.9	30.0	43.8	18.2	14.0	14.3	53.1	20.7	30.8	9.5	61.5	41.7
Banking/Credit Agencies	93.8	88.9	68.2	36.7	37.5	27.3	27.9	23.8	37.5	10.3	30.8	19.0	46.2	33.3
Insurance Carriers	87.5	88.9	86.4	36.7	50.0	27.3	30.2	28.6	62.5	24.1	23.1	9.5	15.4	0.0
FIRE Agents and Brokers	100.0	94.4	81.8	33.3	31.2	9.1	7.0	4.8	53.1	24.1	30.8	14.3	92.3	66.7
Business/Professional Services	100.0	100.0	86.4	16.7	62.5	27.3	9.3	19.0	56.2	17.2	46.2	14.3	61.5	25.0
Nonprofit Services	43.8	16.7	31.8	50.0	50.0	63.6	65.1	20.6	31.2	41.4	23.1	38.1	15.4	58.3
Health Services	50.0	16.7	27.3	43.3	31.2	90.9	60.5	33.3	25.0	48.3	30.8	47.6	38.5	58.3
Educational Services	75.0	44.4	54.5	43.3	50.0	54.5	44.2	52.4	37.5	27.6	38.5	9.5	15.4	8.3
Social Services/Organizations	31.2	27.8	54.5	53.3	37.5	36.4	53.5	42.9	43.8	34.5	30.8	28.6	7.7	50.0
Consumer Services	62.5	66.7	45.5	56.7	0.0	9.1	18.6	28.6	28.1	27.6	69.2	33.3	100.0	91.7
Government/Services														
Federal	31.2	33.3	50.0	33.3	12.5	27.3	20.9	23.8	59.4	44.8	100.0	95.2	23.1	16.7
Military	18.8	22.2	50.0	40.0	25.0	18.2	30.2	14.3	46.9	37.9	100.0	90.5	53.8	25.0
State and Local	0.0	5.6	22.7	43.3	0.0	54.5	44.2	14.3	81.2	96.6	38.5	42.9	30.8	41.7
Administration/Auxiliary	100.0	94.4	72.7	43.3	93.8	45.5	16.3	38.1	31.2	10.3	15.4	4.8	30.8	0.0

Note: For definitions of type/size group codes, see note 3 to chapter 2.

Source: County Business Patterns.

TABLE 2.4

Group Location Quotients (LQ): All High-Tech Industries (High-Tech Manufacturing and High-Tech Services Combined), 1997;
Distribution of Metros (by Quintile): All High-Tech Industry LQs, 1997;
Group LQs: High-Tech Manufacturing and High-Tech Services, 1997

Industrial Category		Number of Metros	All High-Tech Industries							High-Tech LQs	
			LQ	1	2	3	4	5		Manufacturing	Services
Nodal	> 2 Million	16	1.37	9 (56.2)	7 (43.8)	0 (–)	0 (–)	0 (–)		1.25	1.45
Nodal	1–2 Million	18	1.26	9 (50.0)	7 (38.9)	1 (5.6)	1 (5.6)	0 (–)		1.24	1.27
Nodal	250,000–1 Million	22	0.91	4 (18.2)	8 (36.4)	7 (31.8)	3 (13.6)	0 (–)		0.93	0.90
Nodal	< 250,000	30	0.60	2 (6.7)	2 (6.7)	9 (30.0)	8 (26.7)	9 (30.0)		0.69	0.55
Functional Nodal	> 250,000	16	1.41	3 (18.8)	5 (31.2)	5 (31.2)	3 (18.8)	0 (–)		1.96	1.08
Manufacturing/Service	> 250,000	11	0.79	3 (27.3)	1 (9.1)	3 (27.3)	3 (27.3)	1 (9.1)		0.95	0.69
Manufacturing/Service	< 250,000	43	0.81	7 (16.3)	7 (16.3)	3 (7.0)	9 (20.9)	17 (39.5)		1.17	0.59
Manufacturing	> 250,000	21	0.70	3 (14.3)	4 (19.0)	6 (28.6)	3 (14.3)	5 (23.8)		1.04	0.50
Government/Service	> 250,000	32	1.31	11 (34.4)	5 (15.6)	5 (15.6)	8 (25.0)	3 (9.4)		0.99	1.51
Government/Service	< 250,000	29	0.77	4 (13.8)	7 (24.1)	6 (20.7)	9 (31.0)	3 (10.3)		0.79	1.76
Government/Military	> 250,000	13	0.89	2 (15.4)	1 (7.7)	4 (30.8)	3 (23.1)	3 (23.1)		0.80	0.95
Government/Military	< 250,000	21	0.35	1 (4.8)	1 (4.8)	2 (9.5)	2 (9.5)	15 (71.4)		0.28	0.40
Resort/Retirement	> 250,000	13	0.87	2 (15.4)	4 (30.8)	3 (23.1)	3 (23.1)	1 (7.7)		0.88	0.87
Resort/Retirement	< 250,000	12	0.75	1 (8.3)	2 (16.7)	5 (41.7)	2 (16.7)	2 (16.7)		0.91	0.65

Source: County Business Patterns.

(table 2.4). For the *group with 1 million to 2 million population* (e.g., Cleveland, Salt Lake City, and Seattle), the respective LQs for FIRE, business/professional services, and A/A are 1.24, 1.17, and 1.48. The high-tech goods-and-services LQ for this second-largest-population nodal group is 1.26, with half of these places ranked within the top quintile (table 2.4). The *group with 250,000 to 1 million population* (e.g., Memphis, Mobile, and Spokane) tends to be somewhat less specialized in business/professional services, although the degree of concentration in FIRE and A/A is high. Group LQs for wholesaling and for transportation, communications, and utilities are relatively high: 1.14 for wholesaling, and 1.18 for TCU.

The smaller nodal places (with less than 250,000) (e.g., Lubbock, TX; Portland, ME; Roanoke, VA; and Sioux Falls, SD) are more restricted in the variety of services in which they are relatively specialized. Average LQs are highest in wholesaling, retailing, insurance carriers, and health services (respectively, 1.12, 1.16, 1.52, and 1.13).

Table 2.3 presents the other set of measures of relative concentration of employment in selected industrial categories: the percentages of metros in each group that rank within the top two quintiles of all location quotients for each industrial category. These data largely confirm the observations that were based on the metro-group LQs in table 2.2. There is a relatively high degree of specialization in FIRE, business/professional services, A/A, wholesale trade, and TCU among the larger nodal metros; and within TCU, concentration tends to be greatest in transportation. Similarly, the quintile measures verify the importance of wholesaling and retailing in these smaller diversified service economies. In addition, they shed light on the importance of nonprofit services: Half of these smaller places rank within the top two quintiles of the array of nonprofit LQs.

Functional Nodal Metros

Functional nodal metros (e.g., Akron, Dayton, Detroit, and Rochester) are production centers that are also heavily specialized in business/professional services and headquarters and other corporate administrative activities (A/A). All functional nodal places are manufacturing centers, except three:[7] Jersey City, specializing in transportation, wholesaling, and FIRE agents and brokers (respective LQs: 3.33, 1.70, and 3.35); Wilmington, in banking and FIRE agents and brokers (4.11 and 1.33); and Hartford, in insurance carriers (6.70).

Because the larger functional nodal metros are heavily specialized in both corporate administrative and production activities, they show relatively high LQs in business/professional services. For the majority of these places, however, FIRE employment tends to be underrepresented. Apparently, a large proportion of financial services for corporate headquarters located in functional nodal metros is procured from outside sources. A number of these metros are specialized in high-tech goods and/or service employment, and the group high-tech LQ is quite high, 1.41 (see table 2.4, and see below).

Only five metros with a population of less than 250,000 were classified as functional nodal. Because of the small number of places, this group was not analyzed in this or the following chapters.

Manufacturing/Service Metros

Manufacturing/service metros are characterized by relatively high location quotients in manufacturing and in nonprofit services. Many of the larger metros (e.g., Ann Arbor, New Haven, and Providence) are centered on old manufacturing cities that are hosts to large private or state universities. This group specialization in education shows up in a relatively high LQ in educational services (non-government-sponsored institutions) and in state and local government services (which include state-run institutions; see table 2.2).

The smaller-size manufacturing service category (under 250,000 population) (e.g., Longview, TX, and Lynchburg, VA) includes 43 essentially manufacturing metros that tend to have sizable employment in retailing and nonprofit services, especially health services (see table 2.3). The group includes virtually all of the smaller manufacturing-oriented places, with the exception of a handful included within the functional nodal group (see above) and the manufacturing group (see below).

Manufacturing Metros

Manufacturing metros with a population of 250,000 or more (e.g., Flint, MI; Gary, IN; Grand Rapids, MI; and Youngstown, OH) show a concentration of employment largely in manufacturing. Group LQs are also above 1.00 in construction, retailing, and nonprofit services, but the percentages of metros ranked in the upper quintiles of these industry categories are not high (only in educational services is the share of metros ranking within the top two quintiles above 50 percent).

Only five metros classified within the manufacturing group had a population of less than 250,000. As noted above, most of the manufacturing-oriented metros with less than 250,000 population that were possible candidates for this group were classified as manufacturing/service because they tended to have above-average LQs in one or more nonprofit services.

Because of the small number of metros with a population of less than 250,000 that were classified as manufacturing, measures for this size-type group are not shown in this or the following chapters.

Government/Service Metros

The government/service metro group numbers 61 places, of which more than half have more than 250,000 population. Metros in this group are characterized by high LQs in state and local government employment, indicating heavy specialization in state and local government and state-run institutions (the LQ for the large-size group was 1.24; for the small-size group, 1.97). Many have a substantial federal government presence as well (see table 2.3). Twenty-one are state capitals (e.g., Columbia, Oklahoma City, Raleigh, and Sacramento), and a large majority host state universities and medical centers.[8] The large-size group shows an LQ of 1.22 for business/professional services, with well over half of these metros ranked in the top two quintiles. Business/professional services, however, are less important among the smaller-size group.

Government/Military Metros

Government/military metros (e.g., Fayetteville, AR; Norfolk, VA; and Pensacola, FL) are economies with a heavy federal government and/or military presence, clearly indicated by high LQs. Although the greatest specialization is clearly in federal civilian or military employment, a large number of the larger government/military metros have relatively high concentrations of employment in consumer services (69 percent are ranked within the top two quintiles).

Resort/Retirement Metros

The 25 metros classified as resort/retirement include a variety of places, most of which are well-known as popular meccas for retirement, amusement, or gambling (e.g., Fort Lauderdale, Myrtle Beach, Orlando, and Reno). Among both size categories, group LQs are high in retail, FIRE agents and brokers, consumer services, and (reflecting very rapid growth) construction.

It seems evident that the nature of employment included within the FIRE agents and brokers classification differs significantly between the large nodal metros and the resort/retirement metros. Among the large nodal metros, the range of specialization of firms classified as FIRE agents and brokers is likely to be very broad, including (among some of the largest metros) the central operations of the important investment houses and major exchanges. Among retirement places, conversely, firms within this classification are likely to serve a more limited clientele that extends no further than the affluent consumers of brokerage and investment services.

For the larger resort/retirement metros, the group LQ for business/professional services is also relatively high; for the smaller ones, it is not. Nonprofit services, especially health services, play an important role in the economies of many of these places, especially within the smaller-size groups.

High-Tech Manufacturing and Service Metros

Because the rather broad industrial categories used in this study do not break out employment data that specifically cover the burgeoning high-tech manufacturing and service segments of the U.S. metropolitan economy, I have made use of the 3-digit Standard Industrial Classification (SIC) codes that were deemed most applicable to such activities. These codes were those used by De Vol in his recent analysis of the impact of high-tech industries on the relative growth of metropolitan areas:[9]

SIC code	Industrial classification
	High-tech manufacturing
283	Drugs
357	Computer and office equipment
366	Communications equipment
367	Electronic components and accessories
372	Aircraft and parts
376	Guided missiles, space vehicles, and parts
381	Search, detection, navigation, guidance, aeronautical nautical systems, instruments, and equipment
382	Laboratory apparatus and analytical, optical, measuring, and controlling instruments
384	Surgical, medical, and dental instruments and supplies
	High-tech services
481	Telephone communications services
737	Computer programming, data processing, and other computer-related services
781	Motion picture production and allied services
871	Engineering, architectural, and surveying services
873	Research, development, and testing services

Employment in the 14 industries was totaled for each metro to provide a single measure of high-tech employment, and location quotients then were computed and ranked for all metros.[10] Breaking down the array of metro LQs into quintiles permits an initial look at the way in which high-tech employment was distributed among the various metros within the U.S. system in 1997:

Quintile	LQ range
1	4.93–1.23
2	1.22–0.73
3	0.73–0.53
4	0.53–0.34
5	0.34–0.08

Clearly, high-tech employment is heavily concentrated among a relatively small number of metros: LQs for the metros falling within the lowest-ranking three quintiles (i.e., the lowest ranking 60 percent) ranged downward from 0.73 to 0.08.

Table 2.4 presents group LQs for combined high-tech manufacturing and service employment, along with a distribution of metros in each group. It also shows group LQs for high-tech manufacturing and high-tech services separately. High-tech employment (combined) is concentrated most heavily in the two largest-size nodal groups (with group LQs of 1.37 and 1.26), and the 250,000-and-larger functional nodal and government/service groups (with group LQs of 1.41 and 1.31). Among the remaining groups, LQs were much smaller, ranging downward from 0.91 to 0.35.

The distribution of metros by quintiles (see table 2.4) sheds additional light. Among the two largest-size nodal groups, 50 percent or more of the metros fall within the first quintile of LQs for all high-tech employment; almost all fall within the top two quintiles.

This is not, however, the case within the larger-size functional nodal group. Although the LQ of 1.41 for this group is the highest of all, only three metros ranked within the top quintile (San Jose, 4.93; Wichita, 2.89, and Hartford, 1.43). We note also that high-tech manufacturing is relatively more important in this group (LQ of 1.96) than high-tech services (1.08).

Among the larger-size government/service metros, more than a third are ranked within the top combined high-tech employment quintile. In contrast to the finding for the functional nodal group, high-tech services are relatively more important (LQ of 1.51) than are high-tech manufacturers (0.99).

Finally, among the manufacturing/service and manufacturing groups, it is clear that a majority of these places have failed—to any significant extent—to attract the more modern, new-technology firms ("new economy"–type industries).

Additional Findings from Location Quotients

Banking

Although concentrations of banking employment are most commonly found in the larger nodal centers (where they are closely associated with legal and business services and with the investment community), banking-related functions may sometimes account for relatively large shares of employment in metros located away from major urban centers. Such metros may be specialized in carrying out back-office activities, such as credit card processing, check processing, and credit management.

The point can be illustrated by listing the 20 top-ranking metros in banking services:

Group	Rank	LQ
Nodal 1		
New York, NY	9	1.68
Nodal 2		
Charlotte, NC	5	1.95

San Francisco, CA	7	1.87
Columbus, OH	10	1.66
Nodal 3		
Jacksonville, FL	4	2.34
Richmond, VA	6	1.87
Des Moines, IA	11	1.64
Buffalo, NY	17	1.44
Nodal 4		
Sioux Falls, SD	3	2.87
Roanoke, VA	14	1.57
Monroe, LA	15	1.48
Victoria, TX	16	1.45
Billings, MT	19	1.43
Functional nodal 1		
Wilmington, DE	1	4.11
Functional nodal 2		
Racine, WI	8	1.76
Manufacturing 1		
Aurora–Elgin, IL	12	1.62
Manufacturing/service 2		
Hagerstown, MD	2	3.20
Florence, SC	20	1.43
Government/military 2		
Salinas, CA	18	1.44
Government/military 2		
Panama City, FL	13	1.60

Only the largest of these places may be regarded as national or regional banking centers, and evidence of the exact functions performed in the remaining places is not readily available. For several of the latter, however, there is at least some anecdotal information. Sioux Falls, for example, is where a large proportion of Citicorp's credit card processing and collection activities are carried out, and Des Moines and Wilmington are generally known to be centers of back-office activity.

Insurance Carriers

Location quotients indicate that the locational characteristics of insurance firms vary widely. On one hand, the great majority of large and medium-sized nodal centers rank in the top quintiles of the array for insurance carriers (see table 2.3). On the other hand, a sizable number of places with concentrations of such employment are not located in proximity to a large financial or business-centered community. It is intriguing that, among nodal metros with more than 1 million population, the highest ranked stood at only 31 (LQ of 2.01) within the entire insurance-carrier array, while the 10 top-ranked metros, all located in other type/size groups, show much larger LQs:

Group	Rank	LQ
Nodal 3		
Des Moines, IA	3	5.85
Jacksonville, FL	9	3.31
Nodal 4		
Bloomington, IL	1	14.03
Green Bay, WI	7	3.58
Functional nodal		
Hartford, CT	2	6.70
Manufacturing/service 1		
Springfield, MA	5	4.24
Manufacturing/service 2		
Wausau, WI	8	5.05
Greeley, CO	10	3.51
Government/service 1		
Utica–Rome, NY	6	3.68
Government/service 2		
Lincoln, NE	8	3.36

Health Services

Health services are generally considered to be a major provider of service jobs everywhere. In considerable measure, this is true. Even for the metro ranked as poorly as the twentieth percentile, health services in 1997 accounted for 7.7 percent of total 1997 employment (see below). For those ranked in the top quintile, health services accounted for between 11.7 and 31.1 percent of total employment; in 1997, the upper and lower limits of health services quintiles were:

Quintile	Shares (percent)	LQ
1	31.1–11.7	3.43–1.28
2	11.7–10.3	1.28–1.13
3	11.3–8.9	1.13–0.98
4	8.9–7.7	0.98–0.85
5	7.7–4.6	0.85–0.50

Clearly, health services are a major sector for the top-quintile metros, providing not only for the needs of their own populace but acting as regional or subregional medical centers as well.

Examination of the list of metros ranked within the top fifth for health services LQs reveals that a large majority of these places have populations of less than 250,000. For these smaller places, the complex of health service providers may be regarded as a significant part of the export base of the metropolitan economy. In 1997, the number and percentage of metros ranked in the top quintile of health services, by type/size group, were:

Group[a]	Number	Percent	Group	Number	Percent
N_1	4	25.0	Mfg_1	1	4.8
N_2	0	0	GS_1	4	12.5
N_3	2	9.1	GS_2	10	34.5
N_4	8	26.7	GM_1	1	7.7
FN_1	2	12.5	GM_2	7	33.3
MS_1	4	36.4	RR_1	1	7.7
MS_2	13	30.2	RR_2	6	50.0

Note: a. See footnote 3 in this chapter for definitions of the type-size group abbreviations.

(The very small groups, FN_2 and Mfg_2, are not shown. There were no top-quintile metros in these type/size groups.)

Various Types of Metros in the Overall Economy

The several types of metros discussed above fall into essentially two categories. On one hand are the nodal places—the diversified service centers. On the other hand are the remaining types, more narrowly focused on goods or services produced and "exported," with each group playing a somewhat different role within the overall economy.

Clearly, the nodal places are the most important in total employment (see table 1.5), with the 34 largest accounting for close to half of total U.S. nonfarm employment. The major role of these diversified service centers may be at least partially understood using the urban theorist's archetype, "central place." Central places provide a variety of services to their own populace and to surrounding areas (hinterlands).

Small central places provide retailing services and relatively nonspecialized business, financial, educational, medical, and local government services, which are frequently purchased and may not be submitted to substantial time or money transportation costs in delivery to the final user. These smaller urban economies reach out to only limited hinterlands. Larger central places provide the same services to their populaces and immediate hinterlands as do smaller ones, but have grown and added higher levels of specialization and outreach to customers in more distant markets.

In this view, the national system of central places is seen as hierarchical. A large number of small central places have spatially limited service markets, a smaller number of somewhat larger central places have somewhat larger service markets, and a small number of very large central places serve very wide markets. The highest attained level of specialization in services tends to increase with the size of a place and as broader markets are reached. In theory, markets do not overlap for services of a given level of specialization: Larger places do not sell to smaller places the services that the latter produce, but only sell more specialized services.

In the real world, there are few if any "pure" central places (except, perhaps, certain villages and hamlets that perform limited retail functions). Markets do overlap, and in practice, as we have seen, some places develop predominantly as specialized production centers heavily focused on manufacturing activities or as centers with relatively heavy concentrations of employment in government/service, government/military, or resort/retirement activities. All of these places will perform certain central-place functions by providing a range of retail and other services to local and nearby residents. At the same time, metros that are primarily central places may also produce some manufactured goods destined for "export" to outside markets.

Thus the nodal places of our classification have at best mixed economic roles, and the same is true of the specialized metros. Nevertheless, the nodal metros demonstrate a relatively broad spectrum of service specialization (even though the smaller ones tend to be specialized largely as wholesale-retail centers). Conversely, the remaining groups appear to be more narrowly specialized, and within each group, metros tend to share certain characteristics of industrial composition.

The Modern Corporation and the Metropolitan System

The theory of the structure of the urban system has been broadened beyond that sketched above by the work of Pred, who has presented an analysis of the development of the metropolitan system that emphasizes the importance of the location of activities of the large corporation.[11] Pred's theory was treated at some length in *The Economic Transformation of American Cities*, from which the following quotation provides highlights:[12]

> Pred sees the postwar era as one in which the large industrial corporations have played a major role in influencing the interurban transmission of growth. General evidence of the importance of these large organizations is found in the fact that between 1960 and 1973 the number of domestic and foreign jobs controlled by the 500 largest U.S. industrial organizations grew by 68 percent, while total jobs grew 36 percent. The record indicates that a clear majority of private sector employment is directly associated with domestically headquartered "multilocational" corporations.
>
> The principal argument is that city system interdependence is increased by growth of the large corporation as a result of intraorganizational linkages. Large corporations typically

have a larger share of resources given over to administrative and office activities. Expansion within a multilocational organization at a subordinate unit or the opening of a new subordinate unit is likely to bring about expansion of the headquarters unit (or other high or intermediate-level administrative unit). Merger activity in particular is likely to result in increased intercity interdependencies, involving the locating of headquarters increasingly in large metropolitan complexes. Pred maintains, however, that the transmission of intraorganizational growth between cities is not restricted to growth of administrative units, but may also involve the flow of goods, services and specialized information among two or more units of a large organization without necessarily affecting the organization's headquarters.

Interdependence may also involve interorganizational relationships. A number of factors have contributed: transportation advances have lowered the relative costs of shipping goods; jet plane and telecommunications have facilitated the movement of specialized information and encouraged the growth of specialized financial, insurance and other services; and new industrial technology has altered production processes, changed location requirements and created more elaborate input-output relationships. In addition, the pressure to adjust complex production organizations quickly has brought about the need for increased coordination within the firm and frequently necessitated the utilization of specialized outside services. Pred observes that though large complex corporations are hierarchical in organization, such organization is not symmetrically arranged in the manner suggested by central place theory. Headquarters may be located in any of a number of places with other administrative units in other places, many but not all being large. The result is a complex linking of cities.

Shortly after Pred's work appeared, Cohen gave further emphasis to the special role of large cities in delivering advanced services to corporate headquarters and argued that "the transformation of the system of cities ought to be analyzed from the perspective of the rise of metropolitan complexes of corporate activities."[13] One of the principal tasks of *The Economic Transformation of American Cities* was to investigate the importance of financial institutions and corporate service firms within the metropolitan system during the 1960s and early 1970s.[14]

Large Nodal Places as Service Providers

Schwartz has compiled more recent evidence of the importance of larger metropolitan economies in providing corporate services.[15] In a study directed principally at determining the role of central cities and suburbs as providers of services to corporate headquarters, Schwartz examined information for 1990 reported by about 5,000 public and private corporations in the *Corporate Bluebook, 1991 Edition,* to determine the location of each corporate headquarters and, as reported by each headquarters, the location of its principal service providers in 13 major service categories. From this analysis, he was able to determine by type of service the number of reported service-provider "linkages" originating in each place, a linkage being defined as a listed relationship between a supplier of a given service and a corporate headquarters user, wherever located.

Schwartz's data show clearly that hosting corporate headquarters and providing services to these headquarters are important functions of major metropolitan economies. Moreover, the data show that corporate services are exported to an important extent, and that a relatively small number of major metropolitan centers are responsible for the lion's share of these exports.

The following aggregated data highlight the role of major metropolitan centers as providers of corporate services.[16] For corporate service providers, the reported linkages were:

	Total	*Top 10 cities*	*Top 5 cities*	*Top city*
Number	34,851	17,652	13,916	6,974
Percent	100	50.6	39.9	20.0

For intermetropolitan ("exported") service providers, the reported linkages were:

	Total	*Top 10 cities*	*Top 5 cities*	*Top city*
Number	13,237	8,485	5,839	3,958
Percent	100	64.1	55.4	29.9

For *Bluebook* corporate headquarters, the reported linkages were:

	Total	*Top 10 metros*	*Top 5 metros*	*Top metro*
Number	4,944	2,471	1,777	751
Percent	100	50.0	35.9	15.2

Clearly, the very largest metropolitan economies are the major providers of corporate services, with New York, the top-ranking city, accounting for a fifth of all linkages, in comparison with slightly less than a fifth accounted for by the next four largest cities combined. Moreover, 13,237 of 34,851 reported provider linkages (almost two-fifths) are intermetropolitan (exported), and New York accounts for 30 percent of these. The next four highest-ranking cities account for only an additional 16 percent of all intermetropolitan linkages.

Table 2.5 provides more detail regarding service linkages for the six largest service-providing metros (all diversified service centers). New York is by far the largest producer of corporate services, with Chicago in second place. It is interesting that Boston, not Los Angeles, ranks third, even though it is much smaller (3,787,600 population in 1990, relative to 8,741,600 for Los Angeles). Like New York, more than 60 percent of its recorded linkages are accounted for by relationships with headquarters located outside the greater metropolitan area (CMSA). San Francisco ranks behind Los Angeles in total linkages but is characterized by a greater percentage (and number) of outside corporate linkages. Presumably, this is due in large measure to its banking relationships. Philadelphia ranks sixth in total linkages but is, nevertheless, a major American metropolis. It is best understood as a center of both private and not-for-profit sector activities.

Table 2.5 also presents 1990 location quotients for employment in selected industrial groups for each of the six metros. These measures, taken together, are the basis of the brief profiles that follow.[17]

New York

For New York, the findings based on service-provider linkages and numbers of corporate headquarters are generally supported by the LQ measures for industry employment. Total FIRE employment (LQ of 2.15) is larger than in the other five metros profiled here. This is true for banking and especially for FIRE agents and brokers, reflecting in the latter the importance of the city's stock markets and financial district. Insurance carriers (LQ of 1.25) are also an important part of the financial sector. The LQ of 1.53 for business/professional services is consistent with the relatively high level of linkages in the relevant corporate services (especially legal services), and the LQ of 1.37 for A/A fits with the large number of headquarters.

New York has relatively the smallest manufacturing sector of any of the six metros, except for San Francisco. Conversely, its transportation and wholesaling sectors appear to be well developed.

New York's LQ levels for health and education services are rivaled only by Boston and Philadelphia, and suggest that the economy's specialization is not limited to the for-profit sectors. Its high level of social/organization services is also revealed by an LQ of 1.26, well in excess of that of any of the other five metros.

Chicago

Chicago's role as a major distribution center with a well-developed financial center and a continued commitment to manufacturing is readily observed from the LQ data. The manufacturing measure (LQ of 1.04) ranks only behind that for Los Angeles among these very large places, and the wholesaling LQ of 1.44 is well ahead of any of the others. Specialization in transportation is high, and the share of transportation accounted for by trucking and warehousing, about 30 percent (not shown), is quite the highest among these large metropolitan economies. All the financial-sector LQs are high, as are the LQs for business/professional services and A/A.

An inspection of the linkage data, however, indicates that Chicago's total service-provider linkages are only two-fifths as large as those of New York, and that it ranks a poor second to New York in every service, even falling behind Boston in several. Moreover, Chicago exports a much smaller share of its corporate services (roughly 47 percent) than do New York and Boston. Finally, the LQ measures indicate that Chicago ranks low among the six metros in its relative specialization in education, health, and social services.

TABLE 2.5

Corporate Service-Provider Linkages by Metropolitan Center of Origin, Number of
Corporate Headquarters, and Selected Location Quotients,
Six Major Metropolitan Centers, 1990

Type of Service	Number of Linkages by Providers Located in:					
	New York	Chicago	Boston	Los Angeles	San Francisco	Philadelphia
Foreign Banking Relationship	257	109	21	36	37	3
Transfer Agent	599	160	122	62	67	4
Investment Bank	1,022	90	22	20	65	5
Master Trustee	201	162	102	25	44	20
Major Banking Relationship	1,470	655	220	251	322	113
Auditors	413	343	180	190	70	148
Actuarial Consultant	207	153	91	70	55	77
Commercial Insurance Carrier	152	95	115	27	35	68
Business Insurance Carrier	417	184	126	107	67	66
Medical Insurance Carrier	364	109	231	53	33	82
Pension Manager	1,129	314	409	193	177	134
Pension Consultant	127	106	54	31	34	28
Legal Counsel	616	278	172	157	85	101
Total Linkages	6,974	2,758	1,865	1,222	1,091	849
"Exported" outside CMSA[a] (percentage)	60.4	46.6	61.2	33.7	49.5	41.7
Number of Corporate Headquarters (CMSA[a])	751	361	176	285	202	171
In Central City (percentage)	43.9	43.8	22.2	37.2	19.3	27.8
Selected Location Quotients						
Manufacturing	0.60	1.04	0.89	1.18	0.49	0.90
Transportation	1.25	1.44	0.83	1.15	1.98	0.85
Wholesaling	1.13	1.44	1.06	1.27	1.04	1.10
Finance, Insurance, Real Estate (FIRE)	2.15	1.38	1.37	1.14	1.86	1.19
Banking	1.82	1.29	1.22	1.13	1.81	1.04
Insurance Carriers	1.25	1.48	1.35	0.88	1.33	1.51
FIRE Agents and Brokers	2.86	1.50	1.32	1.17	2.14	1.11
Business/Professional Services	1.53	1.39	1.49	1.36	1.78	1.32
Health Services	1.26	0.97	1.26	0.85	0.76	1.28
Educational Services	1.99	0.95	3.29	1.16	1.01	1.87
Social Services/Organizations	1.26	0.94	1.05	0.77	1.04	1.19
Consumer Services	0.93	0.99	0.81	1.58	1.32	0.81
Federal Government	0.71	0.69	0.77	0.59	1.16	1.23
State and Local Government	1.04	0.73	0.76	0.78	0.74	0.74
Administration/Auxiliary	1.37	1.62	1.69	1.01	1.08	1.24

Notes: Schwartz data (see source note below) are for central cities. Location-quotient data are for metropolitan areas (MSA or PMSA). Data should be roughly comparable because central cities dominate their metros in the provision of corporate services.

a. "CMSA" is Consolidated Metropolitan Statistical Area.

Source: Provider linkages and headquarters data are from Alex Schwartz, "Cities and Suburbs as Corporate Service Centers" (final report to the U.S. Economic Development Administration, Washington, D.C., June 1993), tables 3.3, 3.4, 4.10, 5.3, 5.6. Location quotients were compiled from *County Business Patterns* data.

Boston

As was noted above, Boston ranks ahead of both Los Angeles and San Francisco in service-provider linkages with corporate headquarters clients. The LQs for various industry groups associated with corporate services and administration are consistent with the linkage measures, indicating a highly developed corporate-services sector: banking, 1.22; insurance carriers, 1.35; FIRE brokers and agents, 1.32; business/professional services, 1.49; and A/A, 1.69.

Several of the remaining location quotients attest to the high level of Boston's nonprofit-sector specialization. With an LQ of 3.29 in educational services, Boston's specialization in private education is the highest among all metros with more than 500,000 population, and its LQ of 1.26 for health services places it alongside New York and Philadelphia, well ahead of the remaining metros examined in table 2.5.

Los Angeles

Los Angeles is significantly committed to manufacturing (LQ of 1.18) for a major diversified-service metro. There is considerable diversification in this sector (not shown), with the strongest commitment to transportation equipment (aircraft and related), apparel, fabricated metal products, electronic equipment, and instruments in 1990.

Los Angeles is clearly a major distribution center (wholesaling, LQ of 1.27; transportation, 1.15), with employment in trucking and warehousing (a subsector of transportation) second only to Chicago (not shown). Location quotients in FIRE and in business/professional services indicate significant specialization in corporate services but less than its West Coast rival, San Francisco. It is also clear from both the LQ and linkage measures that it is less important as a banking center.

San Francisco

San Francisco is heavily specialized in FIRE and business/professional service activities, with LQs in banking of 1.81; insurance carriers, 1.33; FIRE agents and brokers, 2.14; and business/professional services, 1.78. This specialization is best revealed in the linkage data for major banking relationships, which show that San Francisco banks have a much larger number of corporate clients than Los Angeles banks, and that roughly half of corporate clients are located outside the metropolitan area.

San Francisco is also a major tourist and convention center. This is manifest in its high LQ for consumer services, 1.32, and especially for hotels, 1.86 (not shown).

Philadelphia

With the fourth-largest population of any metro (4.8 million in 1990), Philadelphia is one of the largest regional service centers within the national system. Its important role as a service center in 1990 was due in considerable measure to nonprofit and government sectors, which together accounted for about 30 percent of total employment.[18] Health services and education services were of special importance, reflecting the presence of six major teaching hospitals and a number of private educational institutions, including the University of Pennsylvania. The government-sector employment included a sizable military presence (e.g., U.S. naval shipyards) and a number of important civilian federal establishments.

Both the linkage measures and the LQs indicate less specialization in corporate services than in the other five major cities. Yet the FIRE LQ, 1.19, is by no means small, and the business/professional services LQ, 1.32, is quite high. Among the FIRE subsectors, the insurance carriers LQ, 1.51, ranks first among these six major diversified service metros. Finally, Philadelphia is the home of a large number of corporate headquarters, with a location quotient of 1.24 for A/A, indicating a high relative concentration for this category.

High-Tech Manufacturing and Service Metros

What is not included in the above discussion is some measure of the extent of specialization of these six major nodal metros in the nine manufacturing SICs and five service SICs that were considered to be predominantly "high tech."

The following count of employment LQs greater than 1.10 for high-tech manufacturing and services (SICs) reveals considerable variation in the extent to which these major metropolitan economies are specialized:

Metro economy	High-tech manufacturing	High-tech services
New York, NY	0	2
Chicago, IL	2	4
Boston, MA	7	4
Los Angeles, CA	4	2
San Francisco, CA	1	5
Philadelphia, PA	5	5
Total number of high-tech SICs	9	5

What seems clear is that New York is the least involved in high-tech industries of all the six metros, whereas Boston and Philadelphia are the leaders.

Notes

1. See appendix A for a brief description of the statistical clustering procedure.

2. These headings differ from those used in the previous study in that the designations "manufacturing/service," "government/service," and "government/military" were substituted for "education/manufacturing," "government/education," and "industrial/military," respectively, because they were more descriptive of 1990 conditions. The earlier classification "residential" was found to be no longer applicable, and the classification "mining/industrial," although possibly applicable, contained too few candidates to be useful analytically. In any event, the analysis indicated that those few places that might have been classified as "mining/industrial" were also candidates for alternative classification.

3. In many tables, and frequently in the text, abbreviations for the various type/size groups are used for convenience (all numbers refer to population):

Nodal $\geq$ 2 million:	N_1
Nodal 1 million to 2 million:	N_2
Nodal 250,000 to 1 million:	N_3
Nodal < 250,000:	N_4
Functional nodal $\geq$ 250,000:	FN_1
Functional nodal < 250,000:	FN_2
Manufacturing/service $\geq$ 250,000:	MS_1
Manufacturing/service < 250,000:	MS_2
Manufacturing $\geq$ 250,000:	Mfg_1
Manufacturing < 250,000:	Mfg_2
Government/service $\geq$ 250,000:	GS_1
Government/service < 250,000:	GS_2
Government/military $\geq$ 250,000:	GM_1
Government/military < 250,000:	GM_2
Resort/retirement $\geq$ 250,000:	RR_1
Resort/retirement < 250,000:	RR_2

4. LQs typically have been calculated for employment because more detailed data were available for employment. They could, however, also be calculated for other economic variables (e.g., worker earnings or output).

5. Specialization involves more than the *quantity* of human resources allocated. It also involves the *quality* of those resources—the level of skill and expertise.

6. It is interesting that 3 of the 16 very large nodal metropolitan areas (i.e., with more than 2 million population) are not by themselves major U.S. cities, but rather are Primary Metropolitan Statistical Areas (PMSAs; see appendix A for definition) that are parts of larger metropolitan areas known as Consolidated Metropolitan Statistical Areas (CMSAs) that center on one of the major U.S. cities. These three PMSAs are Nassau–Suffolk (New York CMSA), Anaheim–Santa Ana (Los Angeles CMSA), and Oakland (San Francisco CMSA). Among the 18 nodal metros in the 1 million–2 million group, an additional 3 (Newark, Bergen–Passaic, and Middlesex–Somerset) are PMSAs of the greater New York City CMSA. These PMSAs, formerly outlying suburban or exurban areas or satellite cities, have clearly taken on important roles within the overall U.S. metropolitan system.

7. Except for Hartford, Jersey City, and Wilmington, functional nodal centers have location quotients for manufacturing ranging from 1.31 to 2.06.

8. With the exception of government-sponsored hospitals, which are classified under "health services," "state and local government" includes *all* employees on state and local payrolls. Consequently, state universities and colleges are included in this classification and not in "educational services."

9. De Vol's study made use of estimates of high-tech output, whereas metro employment is examined here; Ross C. De Vol, *America's high tech economy: growth, development, and risks for metropolitan areas* (Santa Monica, CA: Milken Institute, 1999).

10. LQs were also calculated separately for the high-tech manufacturing and high-tech service industries (see table 2.4).

11. Allan Pred, *City systems in advanced economies* (New York, NY: Halsted Press, 1977).

12. The quotation is from T. J. Noyelle and T. M. Stanback Jr., *The economic transformation of American cities* (Totowa, NJ: Rowman and Allanheld, 1983), 34–35. When this excerpt was written, the largest 500 corporations as reported by *Fortune* magazine were manufacturing firms. Although very large service corporations now appear on the list of the 500 largest, the general point that these corporations are multilocational in organization still holds today.

13. Robert Cohen, "The internationalization of capital and U.S. cities," Ph.D. dissertation, New School for Social Research, New York, 1979.

14. See Noyelle and Stanback, *The economic transformation of American cities*, chap. 6.

15. Alex Schwartz, "Cities and suburbs as corporate service centers," final report to U.S. Economic Development Administration, Washington, DC, June 1993.

16. These data are for central cities rather than entire PMSAs or MSAs. Because central cities dominate the PMSA or MSA, the findings are applicable here. In fact, Schwartz's data underestimate the importance of leading metropolitan economies as exporters of corporate services.

17. These profiles are based on employment measures for 1990.

18. The information on shares in this profile is based on the same *County Business Patterns* data used throughout this study, but is not shown in table 2.5.

3

The Export Base and the Growth Process

The Export-Base Model

As Edwin Mills noted in his introduction to *Sources of Metropolitan Growth*,[1]

> The traditional theory of metropolitan growth is the export base model: exports to purchasers outside the metropolitan area drive the local economy. This truism has been used many times in forms that range from very simple Keynesian multiplier models to very complex Leontief input–output models.

Metropolitan areas are very open economies that must provide through exports—to a much greater extent than national economies—a stream of income to pay for imports of goods and services from the outside world. These exports may be generated not only by manufacturers but also by a variety of institutions. These institutions include universities, hospitals, and government installations; firms and institutions producing a range of sophisticated business and professional services; corporate headquarters and administrative offices; and producers of resort/retirement services for visitors or in-migrants.

Growth in the metropolitan economy may be sparked by an increase of the export sector, but it may also be stimulated by a decrease in imports resulting from "import substitution." Suppliers of metro firms previously located elsewhere may enter the area to be close to their customer firms. The likelihood of this occurring increases when customer firms increase in number or size. The concept of import substitution is also applicable to a variety of consumer services, which formerly may have been procured from outside the metro sources but now may be available from local firms that are becoming more competitive because of economies arising out of larger market size or for other reasons.

It is important to note three points about this local growth. First, as export expansion or import substitution gives rise to increased employment and money income, there will be an increase in local-sector demand—an increase in the demand for goods in retail stores, locally produced services such as those provided in restaurants, nonprofit services, and a variety of services provided by municipal government. The effect on employment of increased local-sector demand resulting from a given increase in exports has been shown to be highly significant, typically larger than the direct employment effect of the increasing exports alone.[2]

Second, there is a reciprocal relationship between the export and local sectors: As the local sector expands, exporting firms may be attracted to locate in the region. The appearance of universities, medical centers, theaters, and other institutions and amenities stimulated by earlier (export-led) growth can, in turn, provide an important inducement for still other (exporting) firms to locate nearby.[3] Climate, increasingly, has also become a favorable locational factor, although of course it is not formally a part of the export-base model.

Third, the quality of the labor force itself may be of even greater importance. Growth may feed further growth if it serves to broaden the array of skills and experience of the overall supply of potential employees available to prospective firms. Both export-sector growth and import substitution may feed on qualitative improvements in the labor force.

The concept of the export base, however, should not be addressed simplistically. In addition to direct exports, there are other important sources of inflows of funds, including the labor of workers commuting to employment outside the region, new investment in buildings and housing funded from outside sources, and receipts from "export substitutes": dividends, interest, rent payments, and a variety of transfer payments, especially Social Security, Medicare, and welfare payments (these will be discussed in chapter 4).[4]

Pred's Theory and Growth

Pred's theory, which was discussed briefly in chapter 2, augments but in no way contradicts the export-base theory of urban growth. Pred emphasized that during the postwar era large corporations have played a major role in the interurban transmission of growth. Expansion anywhere within a multilocational corporate organization is likely to bring about growth of the headquarters unit and other administrative units.

Accordingly, those places that already host part of the administrative apparatus of a large corporation are likely to experience both export-sector growth and induced growth in the local sector (or among related service providers). In short, the growth of large corporations affects the metropolitan system at multiple points but is highly likely to favor places that already have established clusters of headquarters or of corporate-service providers.

Neoclassical Growth Theory

The export-base model does not in itself explain how or why firms are prompted to enter the metropolitan economy or to expand. The leading theory dealing with this growth process is *neoclassical growth* theory, which emphasizes the importance of supply-side factors in providing a metropolitan area with the capacity to respond to the demand for its exports.[5] Growth is dependent on the quantity and quality of labor and capital and on technical knowledge. This approach emphasizes the importance of *agglomeration economies*, which may be of two types: *localization* economies and *urbanization* economies. Localization economies are economies for individual firms that "are industry-specific and result from the expansion of a particular industry in a certain place . . . ."[6] Urbanization economies arise "from the greater array of services and opportunities available in larger places. . . ."[7] The principal thrust of this theoretical argument is that agglomeration generates economies of one or both types—leading to the entry of new firms or to the expansion of established ones. In short, growth leads to further growth.

Growth and Economic Specialization

In chapter 2, metropolitan economies were grouped on the basis of similarity of industrial composition of employment and classified in terms of economic (i.e., industrial) specialization. Specialization was equated with disproportionate size (i.e., share) of employment in one or more industrial categories.

Specialization so defined is the outcome of the very same agglomeration economies described briefly above. Some exports from a given metropolitan economy may originate in firms that offer unique products or services and are not part of an industrial category with a high LQ. In general, however, the categories that make up the major export base are likely to have grown to a dominant position by a series of cumulative, interacting processes made possible by virtue of common supplier firms, an experienced labor supply, shared training initiatives, specialized and professionalized services, or a favorable market hinterland. Moreover, the same general principles apply to both diversified service (i.e., nodal) and more narrowly specialized metros (e.g., manufacturing, functional nodal, and resort/retirement).

Factors Retarding Growth

Just as some factors work for the growth of the metropolitan economy, other factors retard growth or bring about decline. One set of negative factors involves rising costs. At certain phases of development, a firm or industry may experience diseconomies from a variety of sources: rising costs of raw materials, labor, or transportation; or a less favorable production-cost structure vis-à-vis rival metropolitan areas and foreign competitors.

Another factor that perhaps has had an even greater impact throughout the period under study is changing technology, which has led to a variety of new products and new production arrangements. For example, the postwar introduction of air conditioning in homes, offices, plants, and vehicles has been a major factor in spurring the shift of industry and human settlement from many older industrial regions to the South and West. New agricultural technology has altered the scale and organization of agriculture and largely shifted its location, significantly affecting the economies of several metropolitan areas that were organized to meet the needs of farmers and of farm-product processors. The revolution in electronics has affected almost every facet of industrial production, transportation, wholesaling, retailing, and finance, rendering some firms uncompetitive or outmoded.

These forces may have limited firms' opportunities for growth, or in some locations may even have brought about reversals in firms' fortunes. But they also have given new opportunities to firms in other locations and to firms with new products and services, in both older and younger metropolitan economies.

Fitting Services into Export-Base Analysis

It is instructive to examine the growth of services within the framework of export-base theory. Unlike manufactured goods—which typically are shipped to customers outside the metropolitan area in which they are produced—services usually are performed for customers close at hand. Thus, the hurdle that most service providers seeking to export must surmount is that their customers deal directly with them—the patient with the doctor, the client with the lawyer, the diner with the restaurant.

Nevertheless, some services are exported, and services (as we have seen) may constitute an important or even the predominant part of a metropolitan economy's export base. To understand how services may constitute part of the export sector, it is important to keep in mind that services may be either *directly* or *indirectly* exported. Services may be exported directly in a number of ways. The service provider may travel to the customer, client, or patient; may maintain a relationship with the customer by mail, telephone, or the Internet, with or without personal contact from time to time; or may be visited by the distantly located customer, client, or patient.

In chapter 2, evidence (the Schwartz study) was presented demonstrating the extent to which several services were provided to corporate-headquarters customers in cities other than those of the providers. But the study also showed that the providers had ongoing relationships ("linkages") with corporate customers located in the same metropolitan area. In the latter case, the provider may be part of the export complex of that metropolitan area, but as an *indirect* service exporter—assuming, of course, that the corporate customer is an exporter.

A variety of service providers may act as indirect exporters in a large, diversified service center. They are likely to range from banks, business consultants, corporate lawyers, and advertising firms to providers of security guards, janitors, and printing. In a major center like Boston or New York, the export base is largely made up of firms that provide services to corporate headquarters. These indirect exporters may account for a major share of export-sector employment.

What complicates the picture conceptually is that firms providing services to exporters (indirect exports) may also be providing them to consumers (e.g., banking and legal services) or to businesses that sell to local consumers (e.g., retailers and restaurants). Nevertheless, the concept of distinct export and local sectors remains applicable: Such firms may be part of the export sector, the local sector, or both.

The above conceptualization is completely consistent with the notion of import substitution. Import substitution may occur because firms or institutions shift their purchasing of goods or services from outside suppliers to suppliers located within the metropolitan economy, and this will be true regardless of whether the firm or institution is part of the export complex or of the local sector itself. Conversely, import substitution may also occur if a consumer substitutes a local for a distant supplier.

Finally—to shed the clearest possible light on the nature of the export base—we need to keep in mind that the role of exports is to provide a stream of dollars that provides the wherewithal for the purchase of imported goods and services. Accordingly, any inflows of dollars from sources other than exports may serve as export substitutes.[8] Thus, payments made by an outside level of government for local roadbuilding or other goods and services bring dollars into the economy, whereas payments made for local services with local tax dollars do not.

Similarly, payment of wages, salaries, and other expenses to run a military base or to operate a university are received largely or wholly from outside, and these activities therefore are largely or wholly part of the export base. Likewise, because grants or philanthropic payments, as well as payments for medical sevices rendered to patients from other metros provide revenues to support a medical center, they must be regarded (at least partly) as an export-sector activity.

Finally, as we have seen, transfer payments and dividends, interest, and rent payments flow from outside the metropolitan economy (although Social Security payroll deductions and pension and other savings contributions clearly offset these inflows).[9] As noted above, these payments are portable for those entitled to receive them, and a net in-migration of persons who spend these payments augments local demand in the same way as does increased employment in a new export industry.

Notes

1. Edwin S. Mills and John F. McDonald, *Sources of metropolitan growth* (New Brunswick, NJ: Center for Urban Policy Research, 1992), xvi.

2. The effect of export expansion or import substitution need not be limited to expansion of local-sector employment. Where there are labor-supply inelasticities, a partial effect may be to increase wage rates.

3. In large measure, these may be considered as "urbanization" economies; see the text below.

4. These payments will, of course, be offset to a greater or less extent by out-payments of dividends, interest, and rent and by contributions to social insurance made by individuals and businesses.

5. Mills considers five theories of metropolitan growth and development: export-base theory, neoclassical growth theory, product-cycle theory, cumulative-causation theory, and disequilibrium theory. Among these, he emphasizes the first two. (Mills and McDonald, *Sources of metropolitan growth*, xv–xxi.)

6. Mills and McDonald, *Sources of metropolitan growth*, xvi.

7. *Ibid*.

8. Of course, tax payments made to outside entities (i.e., state and federal governments) offset such dollar inflows.

9. The earnings data analyzed in this study were published by the U.S. Bureau of Economic Analysis (BEA) net of payroll deductions, so the transfer-payment data analyzed do not require adjustment. This is not, however, necessarily true of DIR. The BEA data do not record the flow of savings dollars into pension funds and the like.

4

The Shift to Services and the
Transformation of Metropolitan Employment

The principal thrust of economic change in the postwar U.S. economy has been a shift from goods to service employment. This development was discussed in chapter 1, and it is shown again in table 4.1, which presents shares of employment by the main industrial categories for 1974 and 1997.

Evidence of Continuity of Specialization

In table 4.1, the shares of U.S. employment are presented alongside the matching industry LQs for each type/size metro group. A comparison of 1997 and 1974 LQs reveals an apparently high degree of continuity in the industrial specialization of metropolitan economies during almost a quarter-century of industrial transformation: For each group, LQs that were high in 1974 tended to be high in 1997, and LQs that were low in 1974 tended to be low in 1997.

Taken together, these measures suggest that most metros continued to play their respective roles during the period. This, in turn, suggests that the rise or decline of a given industry affected the fortunes of some groups of metros more than others. For example, the manufacturing-oriented groups would have tended to face the problems of an eroding export base, as would have government/military groups. Conversely, those groups specializing in, say, banking or wholesaling would not have faced overall negative trends. Metros specializing in business/professional services or health services that maintained or strengthened these specializations would—other things being equal—have been especially favored.

TABLE 4.1
U.S. Distribution (Percentage) of Employment, 1974 and 1997; Employment Location Quotients, 1974 and 1997

Industrial Category	Shares (Percentage) of Total U.S. Employment[a]		Location Quotients							
			Nodal 1		Nodal 2		Nodal 3		Nodal 4	
	1974	1997	1974	1997	1974	1997	1974	1997	1974	1997
Construction	4.95	4.38	1.06	0.91	0.97	1.02	1.04	1.06	0.93	1.07
Manufacturing	25.47	14.81	0.95	0.85	0.97	0.93	0.96	0.90	0.83	0.86
Transportation, Communications, and Utilities	5.07	4.96	1.20	1.17	1.43	1.34	1.01	1.18	1.27	1.04
Transportation	2.74	3.02	1.30	1.21	1.57	1.40	0.99	1.14	1.33	1.08
Communications and Utilities	2.33	1.79	1.04	1.10	1.25	1.19	1.02	1.05	1.21	1.03
Wholesale Trade	5.56	5.41	1.20	1.23	1.26	1.28	1.18	1.14	1.27	1.12
Retail Trade	15.51	17.49	0.97	0.89	0.99	0.97	1.03	1.03	1.18	1.16
Finance, Insurance, and Real Estate (FIRE)	5.43	5.85	1.39	1.34	1.21	1.24	1.14	1.21	0.89	0.98
Banking/Credit Agencies	2.08	2.09	1.20	1.20	1.12	1.18	1.07	1.20	0.94	0.97
Insurance Carriers	1.42	1.24	1.43	1.23	1.38	1.42	1.39	1.67	1.08	1.52
FIRE Agents and Brokers	1.93	2.45	1.54	1.51	1.14	1.18	1.01	1.00	0.70	0.74
Business/Professional Services	3.69	9.75	1.51	1.35	1.26	1.17	0.95	1.01	0.74	0.77
Nonprofit Services	7.80	14.37	1.11	1.04	0.96	0.93	0.99	1.03	1.10	1.10
Health Services	4.61	9.02	1.07	0.99	0.98	0.93	0.99	1.03	1.22	1.13
Educational Services	1.18	1.74	1.43	1.41	0.86	0.87	0.91	0.93	0.68	0.93
Social Services/Organizations	2.01	3.61	1.01	0.99	0.98	0.96	1.03	1.08	1.06	1.10
Consumer Services	3.88	5.20	1.00	1.05	1.02	0.97	0.98	0.90	1.03	0.98
Government/Services										
Federal	3.63	2.24	0.81	0.83	0.87	0.87	0.86	0.92	0.56	0.66
Military	3.42	1.72	0.47	0.44	0.52	0.46	0.99	0.99	0.57	0.60
State and Local	14.74	13.35	0.86	0.82	0.83	0.83	0.95	0.87	1.02	1.00
Total	100.00	100.00								
Administration/Auxiliary	2.83	2.64	1.50	1.36	1.31	1.48	1.03	1.34	0.47	0.80

TABLE 4.1 (continued)

U.S. Distribution (Percentage) of Employment, 1974 and 1997; Employment Location Quotients, 1974 and 1997

Industrial Category	Location Quotients									
	Functional Nodal 1		Manufacturing Services 1		Manufacturing Services 2		Manufacturing 1		Government/ Services 1	
	1974	1997	1974	1997	1974	1997	1974	1997	1974	1997
Construction	1.05	0.95	1.01	0.86	0.95	1.04	1.03	1.07	1.11	1.10
Manufacturing	1.42	1.45	1.31	1.22	1.34	1.39	1.58	1.55	0.53	0.61
Transportation, Communications, and Utilities	0.83	0.87	0.86	0.77	0.98	0.83	0.83	0.82	0.86	0.84
Transportation	0.86	0.90	0.70	0.73	0.82	0.81	0.84	0.82	0.66	0.73
Communications and Utilities	0.76	0.85	1.09	0.85	1.20	0.92	0.84	0.85	1.04	1.07
Wholesale Trade	0.92	1.06	0.81	0.76	0.79	0.81	0.82	0.99	0.83	0.81
Retail Trade	0.95	0.96	1.00	1.03	1.03	1.10	0.99	1.09	1.00	0.98
Finance, Insurance, and Real Estate (FIRE)	0.97	1.01	0.74	0.78	0.65	0.67	0.63	0.69	0.90	0.92
Banking/Credit Agencies	0.84	0.97	0.87	0.78	0.80	0.85	0.79	0.82	0.80	0.83
Insurance Carriers	1.43	1.37	0.60	1.12	0.55	0.67	0.58	0.72	0.87	1.11
FIRE Agents and Brokers	0.69	0.85	0.67	0.64	0.49	0.55	0.50	0.57	0.91	0.91
Business/Professional Services	0.93	1.10	0.75	0.76	0.54	0.67	0.57	0.71	1.15	1.22
Nonprofit Services	0.99	0.98	1.16	1.28	1.08	1.10	0.98	1.01	1.04	1.01
Health Services	1.04	0.97	1.16	1.30	1.19	1.13	1.08	1.04	0.91	0.93
Educational Services	0.94	1.08	1.42	1.68	0.86	1.00	0.63	0.80	1.24	1.10
Social Services/Organizations	0.89	0.93	1.00	1.03	0.97	1.08	0.93	1.03	1.21	1.17
Consumer Services	0.82	0.78	0.80	0.78	0.83	0.81	0.78	0.96	0.97	0.89
Government/Services										
Federal	0.57	0.64	0.59	0.79	0.51	0.61	0.51	0.58	2.84	2.31
Military	0.43	0.42	0.60	0.68	0.47	0.52	0.48	0.56	1.38	1.18
State and Local	0.82	0.79	1.00	1.10	0.99	1.05	0.79	0.82	1.35	1.24
Total										
Administration/Auxiliary	1.81	1.77	0.65	0.83	0.39	0.48	0.51	0.64	0.67	0.79

TABLE 4.1 (continued)

U.S. Distribution (Percentage) of Employment, 1974 and 1997; Employment Location Quotients, 1974 and 1997

Industrial Category	Location Quotients									
	Government/Services 2		Government/Military 1		Government/Military 2		Resort/Retirement 1		Resort/Retirement 2	
	1974	*1997*	*1974*	*1997*	*1974*	*1997*	*1974*	*1997*	*1974*	*1997*
Construction	0.96	1.04	0.99	1.08	0.83	0.92	1.52	1.31	1.57	1.44
Manufacturing	0.58	0.62	0.50	0.63	0.50	0.66	0.51	0.54	0.66	0.55
Transportation, Communications,										
and Utilities	0.77	0.70	0.68	0.78	0.68	0.60	1.01	0.92	1.04	0.83
Transportation	0.61	0.62	0.64	0.74	0.62	0.54	0.74	0.94	0.89	0.83
Communications and Utilities	0.99	0.87	0.74	0.88	0.78	0.75	1.38	0.92	1.25	0.90
Wholesale Trade	0.68	0.58	0.63	0.76	0.67	0.60	0.83	0.90	0.75	0.74
Retail Trade	1.07	1.08	0.92	0.99	0.93	1.07	1.31	1.15	1.27	1.33
Finance, Insurance, and Real Estate										
(FIRE)	0.95	0.76	0.70	0.81	0.59	0.59	1.03	0.97	0.83	0.81
Banking/Credit Agencies	0.87	0.73	0.76	0.84	0.78	0.76	1.04	0.91	0.98	0.81
Insurance Carriers	1.47	0.91	0.53	0.75	0.43	0.32	0.59	0.64	0.31	0.29
FIRE Agents and Brokers	0.63	0.71	0.76	0.81	0.51	0.59	1.34	1.21	1.01	1.10
Business/Professional Services	0.66	0.70	0.74	0.95	0.44	0.57	1.15	1.27	0.75	0.83
Nonprofit Services	0.90	1.05	0.77	0.91	0.67	0.94	0.94	0.92	1.14	1.10
Health Services	0.93	1.12	0.84	0.94	0.76	1.06	1.02	1.00	1.47	1.28
Educational Services	0.40	0.62	0.54	0.72	0.33	0.40	0.75	0.57	0.24	0.40
Social Services/Organizations	1.12	1.09	0.76	0.94	0.68	0.92	0.85	0.87	0.91	0.98
Consumer Services	1.02	0.85	0.97	1.05	0.86	0.83	2.20	2.09	2.31	1.95
Government/Services										
Federal	1.07	0.89	2.66	2.10	2.65	2.47	0.73	0.67	0.59	0.56
Military	0.82	0.68	6.34	5.85	6.81	8.24	1.12	0.73	0.77	0.46
State and Local	2.01	1.97	0.87	0.99	0.98	1.07	1.00	0.88	1.13	0.98
Total										
Administration/Auxiliary	0.27	0.36	0.34	0.51	0.16	0.24	0.45	0.78	0.34	0.30

Note: a. Mining omitted.   *Source: County Business Patterns.*

Job Decreases and Increases

These, however, are at best very rough measures that provide only an initial insight into the way the national transformation has been reflected in the employment structure of individual metropolitan economies. A second set of observations involves measures of how much employment change in each industry has contributed to (or worked against) the growth process. The measures used here are simply the gains in individual metro employment ("job increases") in each industry for which there is growth during the period, calculated separately from the losses in employment ("job decreases") in each industry for which there are declines. By calculating job increases and decreases separately, it is possible to determine the extent to which overall net growth is enhanced by expanding sectors or retarded by declining sectors. Moreover, it is possible to calculate the share of total job increases (or decreases) accounted for by each industrial category within a metro or group.

The Importance of Job Decreases, 1990–97

Not surprisingly, job decreases were highest relative to job increases for those metro groups whose growth rates were lowest (table 4.2). For the very large-size nodal group, job decreases were 46 percent of job increases; and for the largest manufacturing/service group, 69 percent. In general, job decreases were highest relative to job increases among the manufacturing-oriented and government/military metro groups.

Job decreases were by no means uniform *within* metro groups, however (see table 4.2). This is evident for the 16 very large (2.5 million or more population) nodal metros. Of these, 5 (Atlanta, Dallas, Houston, Minneapolis–Saint Paul, and Phoenix) had decreases that were less than 5 percent of increases. The remaining 11 had decreases that were more than 25 percent of increases. In 3 of these 11 (Los Angeles, Nassau–Suffolk, and New York), decreases were greater than increases.

The job-decrease and -increase measures also shed light on the growth characteristics of certain of the relatively fast-growing groups. For 47 percent of the small nodal metros, 48 percent of the small government/service places, and 78 percent of the government/service places with more than 250,000 population, decreases were less than 5 percent of increases. In short, these metros were largely unburdened by declining sectors.

In the groups whose job decreases were largest, the losses were due principally to employment declines in manufacturing. The share of total 1990–97 decreases accounted for by this industrial sector was 45 percent for the largest-size nodal group and ranged from 48 to 63 percent among the four manufacturing-oriented groups (table 4.3). In the two government/military groups, however, where job decreases were also relatively large, the decreases occurred mainly in two related industrial categories, the federal government and the military. Taken

TABLE 4.2
Rates of Growth, Ratios of Job Decreases to Job Increases (JD/JI), and Distribution of Metros by JD/JI Bracket;
by Type /Size Metro Group, 1990–97

Type/Size Group	Growth Rate	JD/JI (percent)	Number and Percentage of Metros by JD/JI Bracket					
			0–0.049	0.05–.099	0.10–0.249	0.250–0.499	0.50–0.999	> 1.00
Nodal > 2 million	0.77	46.1	5 (31.2)	0 —	0 —	4 (25.0)	4 (25.0)	3 (18.8)
Nodal 1–2 million	1.69	16.9	3 (16.7)	4 (22.2)	5 (27.8)	3 (16.7)	1 (5.6)	2 (11.1)
Nodal 250,000–1 million	1.82	16.0	6 (27.3)	3 (13.6)	8 (36.4)	2 (9.1)	1 (4.5)	2 (9.1)
Nodal < 250,000	2.46	7.3	14 (46.7)	6 (20.0)	4 (13.3)	6 (20.0)	0 —	0 —
Functional Nodal > 250,000	1.05	29.3	3 (18.8)	0 —	3 (18.8)	5 (31.2)	4 (25.0)	1 (6.2)
Manufacturing/Service > 250,000	0.33	68.9	1 (9.1)	0 —	2 (18.2)	3 (27.3)	1 (9.1)	4 (36.4)
Manufacturing/Service < 250,000	1.59	23.4	10 (23.3)	6 (14.0)	7 (16.3)	9 (20.9)	5 (11.6)	6 (14.0)
Manufacturing > 250,000	1.26	29.9	4 (19.0)	2 (9.5)	5 (23.8)	5 (23.8)	2 (9.5)	3 (14.8)
Government/Service > 250,000	1.68	19.4	25 (78.1)	3 (9.4)	3 (9.4)	1 (3.1)	0 —	0 —
Government/Service < 250,000	2.18	10.0	14 (48.3)	3 (10.3)	8 (27.6)	2 (6.9)	1 (3.4)	1 (3.4)
Government/Military > 250,000	1.31	36.7	3 (23.1)	1 (7.7)	4 (30.8)	0 —	4 (30.8)	1 (7.7)
Government/Military < 250,000	1.73	27.6	6 (28.6)	5 (23.8)	2 (9.5)	3 (14.3)	4 (19.0)	1 (4.8)
Resort/Retirement > 250,000	2.59	11.3	3 (23.1)	1 (7.7)	5 (38.5)	2 (15.4)	1 (7.7)	1 (7.7)
Resort/Retirement < 250,000	2.44	13.4	3 (25.0)	0 —	6 (50.0)	1 (8.3)	2 (16.7)	0 —

Note: a. In each column, number is followed by percentage in parentheses.
Source: *County Business Patterns.*

together, these two categories accounted for more than 70 percent of all decreases in each of these two size groups of government/military metros.

These data raise questions about the extent to which those metropolitan economies that were hardest hit by job decreases have been able to adjust. For many in the manufacturing-oriented groups, heavy losses of manufacturing employment strongly suggest severe erosion of what was, for these highly specialized economies, the principal export base. Similarly, the closing of military bases seriously damaged the export base of a number of metros in the government/military group.

Yet, paradoxically, only a handful of these metros (6 out of 125 manufacturing-oriented places) showed a net decline in total employment during the 1990–97 period.[1] How are we to account for growth in employment (however modest) in so many places whose export base—or what appears to be the export base—declined? Do income flows from sources other than the traditional export base sustain the metropolitan economy?

In the sections that follow, we first discover which services have created the most jobs. Second, we inquire into the ways each may have come to play a role in the metropolitan export sector. (In chapter 5, we will examine how other income flows help to stimulate or sustain metropolitan economies.)

What Industries Have Created the Most Jobs?

Three industrial categories—retail trade, business/professional services (including some high-tech services), and nonprofit services—accounted for the lion's share of total metropolitan job increases during both periods (table 4.4). Although each was important, trends differed among these service categories, as did the factors affecting demand.

Retail Trade

The strong growth in retail trade during the period 1974–90 reflects a general expansion of the role of retailers, restaurants, and other eating places throughout the country as the sector's share of U.S. employment rose from 15.5 to 17.5 percent. Behind this expansion lay a revolution involving a broadening in the variety of merchandise carried, the development of new types of stores, and the proliferation of franchised outlets (especially fast food outlets), coupled with dramatic changes in retail demand. This growth continued during the 1990s, but at a reduced pace, and retailing accounted for a smaller—but nevertheless major—share of job increases.

Retailing accounted for the largest shares of job creation in the smaller-size groups of metros. This is apparent in table 4.5. Among these size groups, retailing accounted for a fifth or more of total job creation in from 27 to 57 percent of metros. By contrast, in only 1 of the 34 large nodal metros (more than 1 million population) did job creation in retailing account for as much as 20 percent of total jobs added.

TABLE 4.3

Rates of Growth; Job Decreases/Job Increases; Distribution (Percentage) of Job Decreases among Industrial Categories; by Type/Size Metro Group, 1990–97

Type/Size Group	Growth Rate	JD/JI (percent)	Percentage Distribution of Job Decreases				
			Construction	Manufacturing	Federal Government	Military	Other
Nodal > 2 million	0.77	46.1	11.6	44.9	7.8	8.4	27.3
Nodal 1–2 million	1.69	16.9	10.5	51.9	13.0	12.2	12.4
Nodal 250,000–1 million	1.82	16.0	9.5	33.6	13.2	21.4	22.3
Nodal < 250,000	2.46	7.3	4.6	11.8	8.7	21.8	53.1
Functional Nodal > 250,000	1.05	29.3	11.8	50.4	6.9	10.6	20.3
Manufacturing/Service > 250,000	0.33	68.9	0.0	48.0	2.9	4.1	45.0
Manufacturing/Service < 250,000	1.59	23.4	13.9	53.9	4.1	7.6	20.5
Manufacturing > 250,000	1.26	29.9	4.3	63.3	5.9	9.5	17.0
Government/Service > 250,000	1.68	19.4	21.7	13.6	29.0	15.2	20.5
Government/Service < 250,000	2.18	10.0	8.2	9.7	20.4	30.0	31.7
Government/Military > 250,000	1.31	36.7	6.4	8.3	24.4	54.5	6.4
Government/Military < 250,000	1.73	27.6	2.7	10.2	31.9	38.9	16.3
Resort/Retirement > 250,000	2.59	11.3	28.8	22.2	5.4	26.9	16.7
Resort/Retirement < 250,000	2.44	13.4	18.4	29.2	6.7	19.6	26.1

Source: County Business Patterns.

Business/Professional Services

The major role of the industrial category business/professional services in job creation can be explained only through the multiple changes in how firms and governments operate and people live and work. An examination of the long list of SIC titles within this category (see appendix B) suggests several lines of causation.

A first line is the rapid growth of subcontracting by businesses and government for needs outside the realm of computers and related technology. Both large and small businesses have increasingly made use of outside providers, ranging from services for buildings, equipment rentals, and employment agencies, to credit reporting, collection agencies, and art and design services.

A second line of causation stems from the meteoric rise in the development and application of new technology—especially a broad range of technology involving computers. Again, much of this demand for new work and new workers has been satisfied not within business or governmental user organizations but by outsourcing or subcontracting. Among the types of service firms in which employment has expanded to satisfy this new demand are those providing data processing, computer programming, software, computer facilities management, and computer leasing and maintenance.

These new service producers are especially significant because many serve not only large corporations but also all kinds of small businesses. Small businesses often have a special need for outside provision of a variety of services, including temporary office staff, data-processing bureaus, credit reports, bookkeeping agencies, computer and office equipment repairs, and mailing and reproduction services. Moreover, private individuals have increasingly made use of many such services, including tax-return preparation, investment counseling, security systems, and pest control.

In addition to the business/professional services discussed above, many of the high-tech services that were classified within the business/professional category (see chapter 2) have made important contributions to employment growth in some metropolitan economies as part of a high-tech industrial complex whose output comprises a wide range of exportable goods and services—not only for computers, but also for computer-related hardware and software, military equipment, and biomedical products.

Table 4.4 shows that business/professional services made major contributions to employment expansion during the entire period—greater during the 1990s, but also 9 percent or more (frequently much more) of total job increases in every metro group during the preceding years. The very high proportion of metros in which the shares of job increases accounted for by business/professional services were 10 percent or more during the 1990s (table 4.5) suggests that many of these services were becoming relatively ubiquitous—including, in all probability, a fairly wide range of services for small and medium-sized businesses, and even for consumers.

TABLE 4.4

Distribution (Percentage) of Job Increases among Industrial Categories by Type /Size Metro Group, 1974–90 and 1990–97

Type/Size Group	Construction		Manufacturing		Transportation, Communications, and Utilities		Wholesale Trade		Retail Trade		Finance, Insurance, and Real Estate		Business/ Professional Services	
Nodal > 2 million	3.2†	3.0††	2.9	3.6	4.8	6.0	6.2	4.1	16.4	9.1	8.9	3.9	20.5	32.1
Nodal 1–2 million	3.0	5.3	3.4	2.2	5.5	6.1	6.6	5.4	19.2	14.3	8.4	6.4	18.3	25.1
Nodal 250,000–1 million	3.0	3.8	1.9	4.2	7.3	5.7	5.2	4.6	20.8	17.0	8.0	7.3	15.8	22.0
Nodal < 250,000	3.1	6.4	2.7	6.6	6.0	3.6	5.9	3.3	19.0	16.8	8.4	4.1	17.9	17.6
Functional Nodal > 250,000	4.3	3.3	3.7	3.6	5.2	3.6	5.7	4.9	21.6	10.2	6.8	8.0	16.1	33.3
Manufacturing/Service > 250,000	4.8	2.6	2.4	3.1	2.5	3.3	2.6	2.5	20.0	12.9	6.4	0.9	13.4	20.0
Manufacturing/Service < 250,000	3.0	6.0	4.9	7.7	4.1	4.2	3.7	4.0	22.8	18.7	5.6	3.2	10.4	16.7
Manufacturing > 250,000	5.2	5.0	2.6	5.9	2.7	5.3	5.3	5.5	25.8	14.5	5.9	2.3	13.5	18.4
Government/Service > 250,000	4.2	4.9	5.4	6.1	4.0	2.9	4.0	3.9	20.7	13.2	6.6	3.3	13.7	24.8
Government/Service < 250,000	2.9	5.8	4.9	3.8	3.1	3.8	2.8	1.9	22.0	17.4	4.3	3.4	10.0	13.9
Government/Military > 250,000	3.4	3.7	5.0	4.3	3.5	5.7	3.8	5.0	23.4	12.2	5.8	2.7	12.2	20.4
Government/Military < 250,000	2.8	5.0	6.1	6.5	3.8	1.1	2.7	2.3	23.7	18.4	3.8	2.8	8.6	13.7
Resort/Retirement > 250,000	4.7	2.4	7.1	2.2	3.3	5.7	4.3	4.8	23.1	12.3	6.5	4.0	12.4	27.6
Resort/Retirement < 250,000	6.4	5.0	5.1	4.6	3.4	2.7	3.7	4.4	28.0	19.6	5.7	1.9	8.7	17.6

TABLE 4.4 (continued)

Distribution (Percentage) of Job Increases among Industrial Categories by Type /Size Metro Group, 1974–90 and 1990–97

Type/Size Group	Nonprofit Services		Health[a]		Consumer Services		Federal Government		Military		State and Local Government		Administation/ Auxiliary	
Nodal > 2 million	23.6†	24.2††	14.8	14.4	6.6	6.5	0.7	0.0	0.5	0.0	4.9	7.6	4.5	1.0
Nodal 1–2 million	21.6	20.5	14.2	12.8	6.0	5.9	0.8	0.0	0.3	0.0	6.6	8.5	5.2	3.3
Nodal 250,000–1 million	24.0	22.8	15.5	15.2	5.1	5.7	1.1	0.2	0.6	0.1	6.7	6.4	5.1	4.4
Nodal < 250,000	23.1	23.6	14.9	15.9	5.8	7.0	0.9	0.8	0.5	0.0	6.1	9.2	5.0	2.5
Functional Nodal > 250,000	25.7	22.6	16.5	15.0	5.1	4.3	0.6	0.4	0.3	0.0	4.6	5.7	6.9	1.0
Manufacturing/Service > 250,000	33.0	36.8	21.8	22.9	5.1	4.7	0.8	0.9	0.1	1.0	8.7	12.3	2.3	5.4
Manufacturing/Service < 250,000	30.0	24.8	18.2	17.1	5.0	4.8	0.6	0.3	0.3	0.0	9.1	9.4	1.9	2.8
Manufacturing > 250,000	27.6	20.8	17.2	15.6	4.9	12.4	0.6	0.2	0.2	0.0	5.1	9.6	2.7	1.0
Government/Service > 250,000	20.8	23.5	13.7	14.2	4.7	5.5	1.3	0.1	0.4	0.3	13.5	11.1	3.0	1.9
Government/Service < 250,000	23.6	24.4	16.2	17.1	4.8	4.5	1.1	0.2	0.5	0.0	19.4	20.2	1.5	1.7
Government/Military > 250,000	21.2	23.2	14.0	14.4	6.3	6.3	1.8	0.2	1.8	2.3	12.0	14.1	1.5	1.4
Government/Military < 250,000	24.9	24.5	17.7	18.2	4.8	5.5	2.6	0.2	5.6	7.0	10.0	12.5	1.3	1.1
Resort/Retirement > 250,000	15.6	19.6	10.3	15.5	13.0	11.4	0.8	0.4	0.4	0.0	8.7	9.4	2.5	1.7
Resort/Retirement < 250,000	20.0	23.0	13.9	17.6	8.6	9.0	1.0	0.3	0.5	0.0	8.6	11.8	1.1	0.5

Notes:

†   First column under each heading is for period 1974–90.

††   Second column under each heading is for period 1990–97.

a.   Health is a subcategory of Nonprofit Services.

Mining and Miscellaneous have been omitted.

Source: County Business Patterns.

TABLE 4.5
Number and Percentage of Metros in Four Job-Increase Brackets
by Type/Size Metro Group, 1990–97[a]

Type/Size Group	Number of Places	Manufacturing				Retail			
		< 10%	10–19.9%	20–29.9%	≥ 30%	< 10%	10–19.9%	20–29.9%	≥ 30%
Nodal > 2 million	16	16 (100.0)	0 —	—	—	10 (62.5)	6 (37.5)	0 —	—
Nodal 1–2 million	18	17 (94.4)	1 (5.6)	—	—	5 (27.8)	11 (61.1)	1 (5.6)	—
Nodal 250,000–1 million	22	19 (86.4)	2 (9.1)	1 (4.5)	—	5 (22.7)	9 (40.9)	8 (36.4)	—
Nodal < 250,000	30	22 (73.3)	6 (20.0)	2 (6.7)	—	3 (10.0)	19 (63.3)	7 (23.3)	1 (3.3)
Functional Nodal > 250,000	16	14 (87.5)	1 (6.25)	1 (6.25)	—	7 (43.8)	6 (37.5)	3 (18.8)	—
Manufacturing/Service > 250,000	11	10 (90.9)	1 (9.1)	—	—	5 (45.5)	3 (27.3)	2 (18.2)	1 (9.1)
Manufacturing/Service < 250,000	43	33 (76.7)	7 (16.3)	1 (2.3)	2 (4.7)	7 (16.3)	19 (44.2)	13 (30.2)	4 (9.3)
Manufacturing > 250,000	21	19 (90.5)	1 (4.8)	1 (4.8)	—	4 (19.0)	13 (61.9)	4 (19.0)	—
Government/Service > 250,000	32	24 (75.0)	8 (25.0)	—	—	10 (31.2)	18 (56.2)	4 (12.5)	—
Government/Service < 250,000	29	27 (93.1)	2 (6.9)	—	—	4 (13.8)	15 (51.7)	9 (31.0)	1 (3.4)
Government/Military > 250,000	13	12 (92.3)	—	1 (7.7)	—	3 (23.1)	9 (69.2)	1 (7.7)	—
Government/Military < 250,000	21	17 (81.0)	2 (9.5)	1 (4.8)	1 (4.8)	4 (19.0)	5 (23.8)	10 (47.6)	2 (9.5)
Resort/Retirement > 250,000	13	12 (92.3)	1 (7.7)	—	—	3 (23.1)	9 (69.2)	1 (7.7)	—
Resort/Retirement < 250,000	12	9 (75.0)	2 (16.7)	1 (8.3)	—	4 (33.3)	4 (33.3)	2 (16.7)	2 (16.7)

TABLE 4.5 (continued)
Number and Percentage of Metros in Four Job-Increase Brackets
by Type/Size Metro Group, 1990–97[a]

Type/Size Group	Number of Places	Business/Professional Services				Nonprofit Services			
		< 10%	10–19.9%	20–29.9%	≥ 30%	< 10%	10–19.9%	20–29.9%	≥ 30%
Nodal > 2 million	16	1 (6.25)	—	7 (43.8)	8 (50.0)	—	7 (43.8)	3 (18.8)	6 (37.5)
Nodal 1–2 million	18	—	4 (22.2)	10 (55.6)	4 (22.2)	—	9 (50.0)	5 (27.8)	4 (22.2)
Nodal 250,000–1 million	22	—	8 (36.4)	11 (50.0)	3 (13.6)	1 (4.5)	7 (31.8)	7 (31.8)	7 (31.8)
Nodal < 250,000	30	8 (26.7)	16 (53.3)	4 (13.3)	2 (6.7)	3 (10.0)	8 (26.7)	10 (33.3)	9 (30.0)
Functional Nodal > 250,000	16	—	5 (31.2)	7 (43.8)	4 (25.0)	—	5 (31.2)	4 (25.0)	7 (43.8)
Manufacturing/Service > 250,000	11	3 (27.3)	3 (27.3)	3 (27.3)	2 (18.2)	2 (18.2)	1 (9.1)	3 (27.3)	5 (45.5)
Manufacturing/Service < 250,000	43	12 (27.9)	19 (44.2)	7 (16.3)	5 (11.6)	5 (11.6)	8 (18.6)	13 (30.2)	17 (39.6)
Manufacturing > 250,000	21	4 (19.0)	7 (33.3)	8 (39.1)	2 (9.5)	5 (23.8)	3 (14.3)	6 (28.6)	7 (33.3)
Government/Service > 250,000	32	4 (12.5)	9 (28.1)	12 (37.5)	5 (15.6)	1 (3.1)	9 (28.1)	11 (34.4)	11 (34.4)
Government/Service < 250,000	29	10 (34.5)	14 (48.3)	5 (17.2)	—	2 (6.9)	11 (37.9)	6 (20.7)	10 (34.4)
Government/Military > 250,000	13	4 (30.8)	4 (30.8)	2 (15.4)	3 (23.1)	1 (7.7)	4 (30.8)	7 (53.8)	1 (7.7)
Government/Military < 250,000	21	11 (52.4)	6 (28.6)	2 (9.5)	2 (9.5)	1 (4.8)	4 (19.0)	10 (47.6)	6 (28.5)
Resort/Retirement > 250,000	13	2 (15.4)	3 (23.1)	3 (23.1)	5 (38.5)	1 (7.7)	4 (30.8)	5 (38.5)	3 (23.1)
Resort/Retirement < 250,000	12	5 (41.7)	5 (41.7)	1 (8.3)	1 (8.3)	1 (8.3)	4 (33.3)	1 (8.3)	6 (50.0)

Note: a. In each column, number of metros is followed by percentage of metros in parentheses.
Source: County Business Patterns.

Yet in those metros with high job increases in business/professional services—certainly those with increases that accounted for 30 percent or more of all job increases (see table 4.5)—levels of specialization were being enhanced. Moreover, the measures shown below are evidence that the relatively large shares of business/professional job increases in the large nodal, functional nodal, and government/service groups owed much to the growth of employment in high-tech services.

High-Tech Services

Shares of group job increases accounted for by high-tech services from 1990 to 1997 are shown below alongside shares of group job increases in the larger business/professional services category, and (for comparison) high-tech manufacturing:

Type/size group[a]	High-tech services	Business/ professional services	High-tech services as % of Business/ professional services	High-tech manufacturing
N_1	12.0	32.1	37.4	0.3
N_2	9.4	25.1	37.5	0.5
N_3	5.2	22.0	23.6	1.6
N_4	2.4	17.6	13.6	2.3
FN_1	10.8	33.3	32.4	1.6
MS_1	4.7	20.0	23.5	3.5
MS_2	4.1	16.7	24.6	2.7
Mfg_1	3.5	18.4	19.0	2.8
GS_1	12.0	24.8	48.4	1.8
GS_2	3.8	13.9	27.3	2.6
GM_1	7.2	20.4	35.3	1.2
GM_2	1.6	13.7	11.7	0.7
RR_1	4.3	27.6	15.6	0.4
RR_2	2.3	17.6	13.1	0.7

Note: a. See footnote 3 in chapter 2 for definitions of the type-size group abbreviations.

High-tech job increases clearly were most important in metros within the largest nodal groups, the functional nodal (250,000 or more) and the government/service (250,000 or more) groups. Since three of the five services included in the high-tech services classification were also included in the more broadly defined business/professional services, it is not surprising that these metro groups were also those in which business/professional job increases were also largest.

But the relationship between job increases in high-tech services and business/professional services is by no means constant. When the level of high-tech services job increases is expressed as a percentage of business/professional services job increases (see above), the percentages range from 12 to more than 48 percent. In those groups in which high-tech services job increases are highest relative to *total* job increases (i.e., the larger metros and the larger functional nodal and government service metros), they are also highest relative to business/repair services job increases, indicating that both high-tech and other business/professional services were playing an important role in the growth process in these metro groups. Among these groups it is the government/service metros in which high-tech services appear to be relatively most important as creators of jobs, with the high-tech percentage only slightly less than one-half. High-tech services job increases are also large relative to business/professional services job increases in the largest government/military group, but the overall growth rate of this group was relatively low.

Nonprofit Services

Table 4.5 shows that during the 1990s the number of metros in which nonprofit services accounted for 20 percent or more of job increases ranged from half to three-quarters among all groups. For many individual places, the share of job increases was much higher than 20 percent.

Among the nonprofit services, health services were by far the most important among the various groups. The number of metros in which health services accounted for 20 percent or more of all job increases ranged from almost a third in some groups to well over half in others (not shown in table 4.5). Conversely, in only 15 metros in the entire continental United States were less than 5 percent of job increases accounted for by health services. In short, health services accounted for a substantial share of job increases virtually everywhere, but were also a *major* source of new employment among a large share of the metros in every type/size group.

The Remaining Industries

Among the remaining industrial categories, the most important were finance, insurance, and real estate; consumer services; and state and local government. The *FIRE* sector, which generally grew fast during the period 1974–90, typically grew much more slowly during the 1990s (see table 4.4). This was especially true for banking and FIRE agents and brokers, which experienced widespread expansion from 1974 to 1990 but sharply reduced growth in many metros during the most recent period.

In these categories, we see the effect of the surge during the 1970s and 1980s in consumer banking, along with the proliferation of new financial instruments and the increasing popularity of credit cards and consumer finance. The slowing down of employment growth in the 1990s (in FIRE shares of job increases) need not, however, be interpreted as a slackening of demand for FIRE products. What we observe in the 1990s is a consolidation of productivity gains, with the attainment of high levels of computer utilization throughout the banking, brokerage, and insurance industries.

Consumer services merit special attention. This industrial category includes a wide variety of services purchased directly by consumers, ranging from trailer parks, auto repair shops, and parking lots to videocassette rental stores and physical fitness centers. Most of these services could have been found in the marketplace of the largest metropolitan area before the 1970s (and many had long been available everywhere). But rising levels of urbanization and personal income, along with changes in consumer preferences, have sparked a broad increase in demand across the entire urban landscape. The relatively large shares of consumer-services job increases in the resort/retirement metros (both size groups) during both periods (see table 4.4) is quite consistent with the maintenance of patterns of specialization in these consumer-oriented economies.

Table 4.4 shows that job increases in *state and local government* during the 1974–90 period were largest in both government/service size groups and during the 1990s in the under-50,000 government/service group. More detailed analysis of the 1990s (not shown in table 4.5) reveals that, among almost a third of the smaller-size government/service group metros, state and local government services accounted for 31 percent or more of all job increases—indicating that these places were strengthening their economic base in these activities.

Manufacturing is examined last because so few new jobs have been created in this major sector. Nevertheless, it is important to determine the extent to which this type of employment has contributed to growth in each metro group.[2] The principal finding is, of course, that manufacturing accounted for only a small share (from 0 to 10 percent) of job increases among a very large majority of metros.

It is interesting that, of all groups, the three with the largest share of metros showing 10 percent or more of job increases accounted for by manufacturing (1990–97) were the small-size nodal group (less than 250,000), the government/service metros (250,000 or more), and the resort/retirement metros (less than 250,000) (see table 4.5). In short, the jobs created because of increases in manufacturing were generated to a considerable extent outside the traditional manufacturing-oriented places.[3]

An additional observation, which is perhaps of greater interest, is that all the manufacturing-oriented metro groups taken together accounted for only 30 percent of 1990–97 job increases in high-tech manufacturing, in contrast to 34 percent by the combined nodal groups and 26 percent by the combined government/service groups (principally those with more than 250,000 population).

The Metro Export Base in the New Service Society

As services have come to play a more and more important role, how well have individual metropolitan economies fared? Can a viable metropolitan export base be maintained as goods production becomes less important as a source of employment and earnings? In which type of metro has the growth of services favored the maintenance or growth of a vigorous export base?

Services and Goods as Metropolitan Exports

For the most part, manufactured goods are produced for export by metros. Modern manufacturing technology typically requires fairly large-scale production to attain economic operation, so goods producers must reach out to a much wider market than the immediate city or metropolitan area. Moreover, manufactured goods are material in nature and are usually readily transported to customers at distant points.

Services, conversely, are immaterial, cannot be transported (with some exceptions), and often require seller–customer interaction. Many services, such as retailing, have traditionally been considered local-sector activities in a metro or regional economy. Some service providers—such as wholesalers or accounting firms—may function as part of the local sector, because they meet the needs of local-sector firms; or as part of the export sector, because they meet the needs of export-sector firms. In some cases, they may deal directly with customers located outside the metro.

Table 4.6 illustrates the variety of ways in which service firms and institutions may operate in the export or local sector of the metro. An example of a service provider is shown for each industrial category, along with an indication as to whether or not that provider operates in the local sector; in the export sector; or "indirectly" in the local or export sector, by acting as supplier to firms and institutions in the metro that operate in the local sector or are part of the export sector.

The classifications are based, for the most part, on general knowledge and are not quantifiable. It is intended, however, that the classifications relate only to important roles, not to insignificant ones. Nine points can help to explain the local, export, and indirect classifications.

First, *retail stores and eating and drinking places* are of course major players in the local sector, but they (along with hotels) may operate as exporters when a metro is a tourist or convention center. Tourism or convention business is frequently a significant part of a metro's export sector today. Hotels are also heavily dependent on business travelers (an export activity), and may in a number of ways provide support to local firms and institutions (an indirect local-sector activity).

Second, *health services* are provided principally to the local populace, but (as noted in chapters 2 and 3) certain medical centers provide specialized services that attract patients who live outside the metropolitan area.

Third, the same may be said of *education services* when colleges and universities train students from outside as well as inside the metropolitan area. These institutions, along with technical schools, also increasingly offer special training in support of large nearby corporations.

Fourth, all the *business/professional* categories of services are clearly classifiable as "indirect," because they provide for the needs of firms and institutions in the metropolitan economy, some of which are in the local sector and some the export sector. Some service firms (e.g., legal

TABLE 4.6
Illustrations of How Various Types of Services May Be Engaged in the Local and Export Sectors

Industrial Category	Service	Local[a]	Indirect[b]	Export[c]
Transportation	Taxis	x	x	x
	Railways	x	x	x
	Airlines	x	x	x
	Port Facilities		x	x
	Airports	x	x	x
	Trucking Centers		x	x
Utilities	Telephone	x	x	x
	Gas and Electric	x	x	x
Wholesale Trade	Wholesaling and Storage		x	x
Retail Trade	Retail Stores	x		x
	Eating and Drinking	x		x
Finance, Insurance, and Real Estate (FIRE)	Banking/Credit	x	x	x
	Insurance Carriers	x	x	x
	Fire Agents and Brokers	x	x	x
Business and Professional Services	Engineering		x	x
	Legal	x	x	x
	Computer Programming		x	x
	Computer Systems		x	x
	Office Temporaries		x	
Nonprofit Services	Health Services	x		x
	Education	x	x	x
	Social Services	x		
	Membership Organizations	x		
Consumer Services	Hotels		x	x
	Cleaning, etc.	x	x	
	Repair Services	x	x	
	Amusements	x		x

Notes: An "x" indicates that the service may be engaged to a significant extent. Trivial engagement is ignored.

a. "Local" indicates that the service is directly engaged in selling to (or providing for) residents.

b. "Indirect" indicates that the service sells to (or provides for) either (1) firms or institutions directly engaged in the local sector or (2) persons or firms selling outside the metro.

c. "Export" indicates that the service sells to (or provides for) persons, firms, or institutions outside the metro.

firms) also deal directly with residents. Finally, highly specialized business and professional services are exported, largely from major metropolitan centers (see chapter 2), whereas certain specialized high-tech services (e.g., computer software) are produced in a limited number of metros (also see chapter 2).

Fifth, the several *FIRE* categories similarly support local firms and institutions, provide for the needs of local residents, and in some instances export services to users outside the metropolitan economy. In the case of insurance carriers, some service establishments are large processing entities that deal almost entirely with an insurance corporate structure outside the metro. Back-office banking activities and credit card processing are also examples of export-type FIRE services.

Sixth, *wholesalers* may serve local firms but frequently distribute outside the metropolitan area. Wholesalers rarely deal with private parties.

Seventh, most service categories within the *transportation* sector can be classified as "indirect," because they serve metro businesses and institutions. Many also provide services directly to residents within the local sector. What must be noted is that included here are many of the key services of major ports (both deepwater and airline) that are strategic export-sector activities of their host metros.

Eighth, *utilities* are quite obviously involved in serving businesses and institutions of all kinds, as well as the general public. In addition, most large utilities cover services well beyond metropolitan boundaries.

Ninth, *government* services—federal, military, and state and local—are classified as export-sector services, but local government, of course, provides services to local citizens and businesses. State educational institutions are largely export-sector activities, but may also provide services to local citizens in the metropolitan area where they are domiciled.

These nine points do no more than make clear that most categories of services may include activities that are within the export sector of some metros. Unfortunately, we do not have direct measures of the extent of export activity at the metro level, because government data are not reported on this basis. For this reason, we must look to such metro indicators as we do have, including employment LQs and job-increase measures. The initial examination of the group LQs in table 4.1 indicated a strong tendency for metro groups to maintain their relative industrial specialization during the period 1974–97.

More detail was provided by the job-increase and -decrease data. The shares of increases accounted for by business/professional services were for most metro groups impressively large. Table 4.5 shows that, in all groups of metros with 250,000 or more population, increases in business/professional services were generally quite high—accounting for 20 percent or more of total increases in many places, especially among the large nodal, functional nodal, government/service, and resort/retirement metros.

More research will be required to determine the extent to which job increases in this industrial category can be seen as generating growth in the export sector of metros, either as increases in exportable high-tech services or in high-level business or financial services. It seems unlikely that purely high-tech services will flourish as part of metro export sectors, except in a fairly limited number of places that offer certain requisites, including the availability of skilled personnel, proximity to a major university, and (perhaps) a favorable climate.

As regards high-level business services, their specialization and export are likely to be confined, for the most part, to the larger nodal metropolitan areas. Some financial services, such as back-office banking and credit card processing, can indeed be provided from decentralized points, as we have seen (chapter 2), and the same is true for insurance carriers and financial advisory and investment services. In general, decentralization of high-level services of all sorts is being abetted by computer and telecommunications technology, and a wider range of locational choices may lie ahead. There is not much evidence, however, that it has proceeded very far.

Taken as a whole, the tremendous growth of business/professional services during the entire 1974–97 period must be seen as largely the result of the enormous groundswell in the use by large and small businesses alike of a variety of independently provided services across a broad spectrum of towns and cities throughout the country. To a large extent, such a generalized increase cannot be regarded as accounting for the buildup of critical metropolitan export bases.[4]

The evidence relating to nonprofit services has been presented, in part, in the discussion of health services in chapter 2. Health services have grown everywhere, but in some metros they have developed to an even greater extent where specialized treatments are administered. In recent years, such medical services have become a very important part of the export sector of a number of metros that have come to function as regional or subregional medical centers. The larger of these centers also have medical schools, which are affiliated with universities. Because in both their roles—delivering medical services and training medical personnel—they are serving an area beyond the metropolitan area where they are domiciled, they are clearly engaged in export-sector activities.

By the same logic, colleges and universities may be an important part of the metro export sector, even though smaller colleges and technical schools typically provide educational services mainly for metro residents. Similarly, social and religious organizations may operate administrative offices that serve an area beyond the metro's boundaries, and such activities will be a part of the export sector.

A Summing-Up

Although the job-increase data do not distinguish employment growth in the export sectors from expansion of local activities, several observations help to explain what has been taking place. First, much of the rise of services has been ubiquitous. There is clear evidence in the measures presented above that, across a broad spectrum of metros, there was a vigorous expansion of retailing employment (at least during the 1974–90 period), business/professional services, health services, and consumer services. Important reasons for this widespread increase in the popularity of a variety of services are readily discerned: changing lifestyles, new consumption priorities and buying habits resulting partly from more participation by women in the workforce, a rising demand for health services, and more dependence by local businesses and institutions on outsourced services.

Second, there is also strong evidence of the building of the service export base in a large number of metros. This evidence is found in the high levels of job increases in certain industrial categories among certain metro groups. For example, FIRE and business/professional services have accounted for sizable shares of job increases in the large nodal groups, which are especially dramatic when we observe buildups in individual cities (e.g., FIRE agents and brokers in New York, business/professional services in Boston).

Third, the shift to services has brought major alterations in metropolitan local sectors everywhere and buildups of metropolitan export sectors selectively. In general, the metro groups most favored by service-type export-sector buildup have been the large nodal, government/service, and rapidly growing resort/recreation places. More detailed analysis would reveal that at least some metros in all groups have benefited. It is quite apparent that new types of specialization are developing—including not only freestanding insurance carriers and financial back-office processing but also research, transportation, high-tech services, tourism, conventions, and (for some places) the very rapid growth of all activities related to retirement for an aging population.

Other Considerations

Upgrading Producer Output

Thus far, export-sector growth has been treated only in terms of the number of persons employed in export-related activities. But there is clearly also an earnings-income dimension. If output is upgraded in the export sector and workers' earnings rise, the flow of dollars into the economy is increased. In chapter 6, measures of earnings will be presented for the various industrial categories, and we will observe for a number of metro groups evidence of significant upgrading in manufacturing generally and in certain service categories.

Import Substitution and the Rise in Local Demand

Import substitution occurs when firms or institutions shift from purchasing goods or services outside the metropolitan economy—"importing"—to purchasing from firms located within the metropolitan economy. The effect is, of course, to redirect an outflow of dollars to providers within the metro and thereby to increase earnings and other returns within the metro. Essentially the same effect can occur if consumers alter their buying patterns to include a larger share of their purchases in the form of locally produced services and goods.

There is considerable evidence that such import substitution and changes in consumption patterns have been widespread. Short-order food outlets and restaurants of all sorts have flourished as a growing share of the consumer's budget has been allocated to food procured away from home. More money is spent on a variety of personal services, such as cleaning, tax preparation, and health clubs, and on medical services and higher education. Further, more retail dollars are spent close to home as malls with their many well-stocked stores bring a great variety of goods within reach of the average consumer.

All this has taken place as a result of a confluence of powerful economic and social forces: the entry of more and more women (particularly former housewives) into the labor market, with resulting changes in the demand for food and clothing; and a greater demand for health services and higher education, coupled with the development of more sophisticated health care delivery systems and the growth of technical schools and branches of state university systems—all bringing critical services to locations closer to the consumer.

For businesses and institutions, there has been a marked increase in the purchase of a variety of services, including janitorial, security, office temporaries, consulting, public relations, and computer programming and maintenance. Although this trend has been partly the result of a shift from providing these services within organizations to depending on outside sources, there appears to be a net increase in local demand simply because of an increased need for services by user firms and organizations.

Non-Earned Income

In chapter 1, we observed that non-earned income (TP and DIR), like earned income, contributes to aggregate demand in the metropolitan economy. In some metros, these income payments may be of major importance, even rivaling earned income as sources of dollar flows to residents, out of which local-sector purchases are made.

Accordingly, in resorts and retirement communities where residents have migrated and are largely, or totally, dependent on social security payments and the returns from retirement portfolios, the level of consumption expenditures of these residents for retail services, consumer services, and even certain financial and business/professional services (e.g., banking, stockbrokers, and legal services) may be heavily influenced by the inflows of nonearned income. The relative importance of these flows among the various metro groups will be discussed in chapter 5.

Other Dollar Flows

From what has been said regarding non-earned income, it follows that dollar flows into the metropolitan economy (from whatever source) may have a stimulating effect. Thus construction of public infrastructure by the states or federal government will result in a flow of dollars into the metropolitan economy. Just how much this flow benefits a given metro depends, of course, on how much demand is created for the goods and services of firms within the metro.

Conversely, taxes and remittances for social insurance are outflows. To the extent that there is a net *outflow*, aggregate demand within the metropolitan economy is weakened; to the extent that there is a net *inflow*, it is strengthened.

Recognizing Inflows and Outflows

In understanding the nature of metropolitan growth and development, it is important to recognize the significance of dollar flows. Chapter 5 will present evidence of the extent to which net inflows of TP and DIR have varied among metropolitan economies. It is unfortunate that similar data for other flows are not available for individual metros, but clearly some places have gained while others have not.

Structural Change and Continuity in Large Metros

New York and Its Nodal Challengers

The LQs in table 4.7 indicate a fairly high level of stability among large nodal metros. Yet it is important to look more closely at what some of these metropolitan economies may have gained by specializing as centers of corporate and institutional services, thereby threatening the position of others at the apex of the hierarchy. Moreover, we need to examine changes in New York's economy that may have served to either strengthen or weaken its special role in the overall metropolitan system.

This is of importance because of the interest of urban scholars in recent years in the rise of "world cities" (cities that perform key roles in international transactions), and especially in New York's competitive position and future as a world city.[5]

Markusen and Gwiasda have investigated this issue in a study that draws on data compiled by other researchers as well as their own new material. They argue:

> The multipolarity of the American urban system . . . acts as a major handicap in New York's struggle for status in a multipolar world system. On the one hand, New York is competing with other major American cities for leadership in producer services. On the other, it is competing for financial as well as business service leadership with the other major capitals of the world.[6]

TABLE 4.7

Large Nodal Metros, Growth Rank 1974–90 and 1990–97; Location Quotients for Selected Industrial Categories, 1974, 1990, 1997

Metro Population	Growth Rank[a]		Banking			Insurance Carriers		
	1974–90	1990–97	1974	1990	1997	1974	1990	1997
≥ 2 million								
Los Angeles	B	C	1.02	1.13	0.99	0.98	0.88	0.87
New York	C	C	1.85	1.82	1.68	1.57	1.25	1.41
Chicago	C	C	1.21	1.29	1.31	2.22	1.48	1.29
Philadelphia	C	C	0.98	1.04	1.05	1.74	1.51	2.01
Boston	B	C	1.05	1.22	1.13	2.00	1.35	1.41
Houston	A	A	0.96	0.88	0.82	0.95	0.81	0.68
Atlanta	A	A	1.24	1.02	1.12	1.17	1.29	1.19
Nassau–Suffolk, NY	B	C	1.10	1.21	1.20	1.22	1.04	1.23
Dallas	A	A	0.99	1.12	1.25	2.30	1.57	1.32
Saint Louis	C	C	1.03	1.04	1.07	0.78	1.01	0.94
Minneapolis	B	B	0.94	0.93	0.96	1.09	1.58	1.99
Anaheim–Santa Ana	A	C	0.94	1.28	1.24	1.36	1.33	1.07
Baltimore	B	C	0.87	1.11	1.05	1.02	1.17	0.99
Phoenix	A	A	1.25	1.07	1.38	0.81	1.00	1.07
Pittsburgh	C	C	1.10	1.19	1.38	0.61	0.80	1.02
Oakland	A	B	0.97	1.31	1.23	0.72	0.74	0.68
1–2 million								
Seattle	A	A	1.21	1.00	0.91	2.61	1.32	1.18
Miami	B	C	1.36	1.44	1.16	0.74	0.76	1.13
Newark, NJ	C	C	0.92	1.08	0.98	1.99	2.30	2.92
Cleveland	C	C	0.96	0.90	1.33	0.68	1.01	1.27
Denver	A	A	1.14	1.18	1.11	0.96	1.19	1.33

TABLE 4.7 (continued)
Large Nodal Metros, Growth Rank 1974–90 and 1990–97; Location Quotients for Selected Industrial Categories,
1974, 1990, 1997

Metro Population	Growth Rank[a]		Banking			Insurance Carriers		
	1974–90	1990–97	1974	1990	1997	1974	1990	1997
San Francisco	B	C	1.35	1.81	1.87	2.61	1.33	1.15
Kansas City	B	B	1.06	1.15	1.18	1.22	1.63	1.45
Cincinnati	B	B	0.90	0.79	1.05	0.93	1.15	1.27
Milwaukee	C	C	0.95	0.93	0.95	1.27	2.37	2.40
Columbus	B	B	0.99	0.85	1.66	2.95	2.29	2.24
Fort Worth	A	A	0.98	0.78	0.71	0.93	0.62	0.74
Bergen–Passaic, NJ	C	C	0.89	0.98	0.94	0.45	0.85	0.81
New Orleans	C	C	1.04	1.00	0.98	0.91	0.78	0.59
Indianapolis	B	B	1.12	0.86	1.09	2.12	1.99	1.64
Portland, OR	B	A	2.15	1.13	1.12	1.07	1.36	1.23
Charlotte, NC	A	A	1.42	1.07	1.95	0.96	1.16	1.15
Salt Lake City	A	A	1.26	0.86	1.27	0.60	0.73	0.81
Middlesex–Somerset, NJ	A	B	0.69	0.91	0.76	0.48	1.50	1.86

TABLE 4.7 (continued)
Large Nodal Metros, Growth Rank 1974–90 and 1990–97; Location Quotients for Selected Industrial Categories, 1974, 1990, 1997

Metro Population	Growth Rank[a]		FIRE Agents and Brokers			Business/Professional Services			Administration/ Auxiliary		
	1974–90	1990–97	1974	1990	1997	1974	1990	1997	1974	1990	1997
≥ 2 million											
Los Angeles	B	C	1.11	1.17	1.04	1.56	1.36	1.32	1.04	1.01	0.93
New York	C	C	3.20	2.86	3.22	2.03	1.53	1.28	1.86	1.37	1.08
Chicago	C	C	1.32	1.50	1.60	1.47	1.39	1.38	1.84	1.62	1.48
Philadelphia	C	C	1.00	1.11	1.17	1.22	1.32	1.29	1.19	1.24	1.32
Boston	B	C	1.16	1.32	1.75	1.39	1.49	1.52	1.21	1.69	1.16
Houston	A	A	1.40	1.47	1.19	1.72	1.66	1.51	2.23	1.98	1.81
Atlanta	A	A	1.47	1.19	1.13	1.64	1.38	1.45	1.65	2.10	2.10
Nassau–Suffolk, NY	B	C	1.03	1.21	1.35	1.49	1.27	1.15	0.60	0.64	0.82
Dallas	A	A	1.60	1.74	1.35	1.46	1.55	1.76	1.76	2.04	2.12
Saint Louis	C	C	0.90	0.94	1.03	1.11	1.02	0.97	1.41	1.56	1.40
Minneapolis	B	B	1.32	1.28	1.24	1.33	1.14	1.20	1.97	2.03	1.99
Anaheim–Santa Ana	A	C	1.26	1.53	1.44	1.36	1.48	1.43	0.83	1.20	1.28
Baltimore	B	C	0.97	1.03	1.14	1.20	1.19	1.11	1.05	0.78	0.88
Phoenix	A	A	1.29	1.20	1.07	1.29	1.23	1.50	0.76	0.93	1.06
Pittsburgh	C	C	0.85	0.91	1.00	1.11	1.19	1.04	2.07	1.46	1.29
Oakland	A	B	0.94	1.00	0.94	1.03	1.26	1.28	1.48	1.29	1.50
1–2 million											
Seattle	A	A	0.98	1.15	1.05	1.04	1.06	1.13	1.08	1.40	1.49
Miami	B	C	2.60	1.56	1.37	1.47	1.22	1.17	0.74	0.91	0.81
Newark, NJ	C	C	0.90	1.26	1.15	1.39	1.35	1.23	2.19	2.18	1.65
Cleveland	C	C	0.83	1.16	1.06	1.50	1.14	1.05	1.60	1.54	1.63
Denver	A	A	1.29	1.43	1.53	1.31	1.35	1.40	1.32	1.03	1.06

TABLE 4.7 (continued)
Large Nodal Metros, Growth Rank 1974–90 and 1990–97; Location Quotients for Selected Industrial Categories, 1974, 1990, 1997

Metro Population	*Growth Rank*[a]		*FIRE* Agents and Brokers			*Business/Professional* Services			*Administration/* Auxiliary		
	1974–90	*1990–97*	*1974*	*1990*	*1997*	*1974*	*1990*	*1997*	*1974*	*1990*	*1997*
San Francisco	B	C	1.74	2.14	2.29	1.77	1.78	1.67	1.33	1.08	1.37
Kansas City	B	B	1.42	1.08	1.15	1.22	1.03	1.04	1.16	1.05	1.05
Cincinnati	B	B	0.88	0.82	0.78	1.12	1.08	1.06	1.65	1.62	1.95
Milwaukee	C	C	0.97	0.90	1.01	1.03	1.07	1.01	0.89	1.00	1.12
Columbus	B	B	0.91	1.12	1.00	1.25	1.23	1.08	1.30	1.74	1.96
Fort Worth	A	A	0.81	0.83	0.83	1.01	0.93	1.07	0.82	1.26	1.90
Bergen-Passaic, NJ	C	C	0.92	1.12	1.14	1.40	1.28	1.25	2.10	2.11	2.60
New Orleans	C	C	0.93	1.01	0.91	1.57	1.21	1.01	1.12	1.07	0.52
Indianapolis	B	B	1.24	1.03	1.11	0.84	1.03	0.92	0.95	0.97	1.35
Portland, OR	B	A	1.02	1.04	1.07	1.07	1.03	1.13	0.84	1.02	2.14
Charlotte, NC	A	A	0.69	0.85	0.95	0.85	0.85	1.08	0.90	1.46	1.13
Salt Lake City	A	A	0.88	0.80	0.84	0.94	1.20	1.09	0.88	0.82	1.06
Middlesex-Somerset, NJ	A	B	0.51	1.26	1.46	0.87	1.24	1.66	1.98	3.11	2.25

Note: a. Growth Rank—A = top third; B = middle third; C = lowest third.
Source: County Business Patterns.

Two general observations can be made. First, in 1990 New York occupied the dominant position as the corporate and financial services center of the U.S. economy. This finding, which was set forth in chapter 2, was based on Schwartz's service-provider estimates, along with related location quotients from this study.

Second, comparisons of 1997 LQs with 1990 and 1974 LQs for key financial, business service, and corporate administrative industrial categories provide at best a mixed picture of trends in New York's specialization relative to other major U.S. metros. Moreover, the data seem to indicate—notwithstanding New York's still dominant position in 1997—that some emerging metropolitan economies were making competitive inroads.

For each nodal metro with 1 million or more (1990) population, table 4.7 presents 1974, 1990, and 1997 LQs for banking, insurance carriers, FIRE brokers and agents, business/professional services, and administration/auxiliary, along with the rankings for employment growth rates during the 1974–90 and 1990–97 periods. We note immediately that—although highest among all the metros in banking and FIRE brokers and agents, and quite high in the remaining industry groups—New York's LQs declined from 1974 to 1997 in every industry group shown except for FIRE brokers and agents (the Wall Street investment sector), where its LQ had risen to 3.22 in 1997. These declines, alongside 1974–97 gains (not shown) in health services (1.07 to 1.31), education services (1.82 to 2.00), and state and local government (0.95 to 1.61), suggest a tilt away from the specialization of the sort that would maximize New York's prospects for continued dominance as a world city.[7]

Table 4.7 provides little evidence of increasing specialization on the part of New York's largest rivals, Chicago and Los Angeles, that would indicate increasing competitiveness, although San Francisco, often dubbed "the Gateway to the Pacific," did show significant increases in its specialization in banking and FIRE brokers and agents and a continued very high level of specialization in business/professional services (LQ of 1.67).

Boston has clearly been an important rival as an exporter of corporate services (see chapter 2). Table 4.7 shows high LQs for each service category. Boston ranked low in growth during the 1990s, however, and there seems little reason to anticipate that it will emerge as a major new threat to New York's position as a national and international service center.

It seems likely that the greatest rivalry will come, perhaps collectively, from the fast-growing "new" regional centers, of which the most important appear to be Dallas and Atlanta. In the Southwest, Dallas is a rising star. It has shown substantial LQ gains in banking (0.99 to 1.25), business/professional services (1.46 to 1.76), and administration/auxiliary (1.76 to 2.12). Atlanta is the largest metropolis in the Southeast, and it is one of the nation's leading centers for corporate administrative offices (its LQ for A/A rose from 1.65 to 2.10 during the 1974–97 period). It may well have increased its competitiveness vis-à-vis New York in some areas (surely this has been the case in recent years in the field of communications). We note, however, that its relative specialization in banking, though high, has declined (with an LQ sinking from 1.24

to 1.12). This is also true in FIRE agents and brokers (1.47 to 1.13) and business/professional services (1.64 to 1.45).

The remaining high-growth large nodal metros are Houston, Phoenix, Seattle, Denver, Portland, Charlotte, and Salt Lake City.[8] Houston, though a high-growth economy, does not appear to be moving toward a highly developed corporate complex; its LQs declined during the 1990s in all the services shown in table 4.7. Phoenix has gained in specialization in banking, insurance carriers, business/professional services, and A/A, but its 1997 LQs are relatively high only in banking (1.38) and business/professional services (1.50).

Seattle has declined sharply in its banking specialization as well as in insurance carriers but has made impressive gains in business/professional services (1.04 to 1.13) and A/A (1.08 to 1.49). Denver shows high levels of specialization in all the service categories examined in table 4.7, but may well be more limited in its future development as a major regional center by its location, far from the burgeoning, heavily populated coastal areas.

Finally, the Portland, Charlotte, and Salt Lake City metros, although smaller (less than 1.5 million population in 1997), are important regional centers for financial and business services. Of these three, only Charlotte has emerged as a significant competitor to New York in any major service category. Its banking LQ of 1.95 reflects its prominence as the headquarters city for the Bank of America, one of the country's leading banking institutions, as well as the home of the headquarters or principal offices of two leading regional banks.

An additional observation relevant to the Markusen–Gwiasda thesis relates to the analysis of earnings. In chapter 5 (see table 5.3), measures of 1997 earnings relatives in the three key industrial categories related to financial and business services (banking, FIRE agents and brokers, and business/professional services) and 1974–97 changes in earnings levels in these services are examined for New York and selected other large nodal metros. The conclusions from the analysis of these measures are that New York ranked first or second in banking and FIRE agents' and brokers' average earnings levels but not in business/professional services. Moreover, New York ranked first in (percentage) increases in earnings levels in banking and FIRE agents and brokers during the period, but again not in business/professional services. These findings—taken together with those relating to LQs (see above)—appear to support Markusen and Gwiasda's general conclusions that New York's world position is strongest in its financial sectors, and most vulnerable in its other corporate services.

Were Large Non-nodal Metros Diversifying?

In the previous section, groups of large nodal places with populations of 1–2 million and 2 million or more were examined for evidence of increased importance in the national hierarchy; but no special attention was given to the developing roles of large metropolitan economies classified among the remaining groups. Yet some of these metros—such as San Antonio and

TABLE 4.8

Location Quotients for Selected Industrial Categories, All Non-nodal Metros with Populations of More than 1 Million, 1974, 1990, and 1997

Industrial Category	Functional Nodal											
	Detroit, MI			San Jose, CA			Hartford, CT			Rochester, NY		
	1974	1990	1997	1974	1990	1997	1974	1990	1997	1974	1990	1997
Manufacturing	1.36	1.33	1.45	1.43	1.85	1.77	1.18	1.08	1.00	1.54	1.55	1.59
Transportation, Communications, and Utilities												
Transportation	0.88	0.92	0.95	0.43	0.48	0.49	0.69	0.93	0.85	0.51	0.53	0.58
Communications and Utilities	0.90	1.00	0.91	0.81	0.64	0.63	0.47	0.86	0.93	0.85	0.79	0.85
Wholesale Trade	0.95	1.06	1.03	0.79	1.24	1.52	0.78	0.97	0.99	0.81	0.99	0.82
Retail Trade	1.02	1.06	1.00	0.96	0.79	0.76	0.86	0.91	0.88	0.91	0.97	0.98
Finance, Insurance, and Real Estate (FIRE)	1.01	0.94	0.98	0.69	0.63	0.51	2.78	2.04	2.14	0.66	0.78	0.72
Business/Professional Services	1.10	1.19	1.26	1.50	1.54	1.83	0.95	1.00	0.89	0.86	0.85	0.90
Nonprofit Services												
Health Services	1.24	1.15	1.00	0.90	0.71	0.66	1.05	1.09	1.18	0.97	1.03	1.09
Educational Services	0.51	0.57	0.53	1.29	1.81	1.50	0.92	1.20	1.14	2.98	2.94	2.45
Social Services/Organizations	0.81	0.96	0.90	0.59	0.69	0.67	0.92	0.94	0.94	0.97	1.07	1.03
Consumer Services	0.92	0.88	0.84	0.79	0.79	0.80	0.69	0.76	0.72	0.71	0.73	0.69
Government/Service												
Federal	0.54	0.58	0.62	0.64	0.54	0.60	0.40	0.48	0.56	0.37	0.37	0.44
Military	0.26	0.35	0.29	0.67	0.47	0.27	0.31	0.29	0.27	0.27	0.28	0.26
State and Local	0.82	0.79	0.72	0.83	0.64	0.58	0.91	0.92	0.97	0.94	0.90	0.97
Administration/Auxiliary	2.70	2.33	2.38	1.10	1.55	1.80	0.82	1.10	0.86	1.45	1.73	1.71

TABLE 4.8 (continued)
Location Quotients for Selected Industrial Categories, All Non-nodal Metros with Populations of More than 1 Million, 1974, 1990, and 1997

Industrial Category	Government/Service									Government/Military					
	Washington, D.C.			Sacramento, CA			San Diego, CA			Norfolk, VA			San Antonio, TX		
	1974	1990	1997	1974	1990	1997	1974	1990	1997	1974	1990	1997	1974	1990	1997
Manufacturing	0.16	0.24	0.24	0.28	0.42	0.49	0.52	0.68	0.71	0.57	0.54	0.53	0.40	0.43	0.49
Transportation, Communications, and Utilities															
Transportation	0.66	0.71	0.66	0.50	0.79	0.82	0.48	0.55	0.60	0.80	0.67	0.71	0.79	0.75	0.84
Communications and Utilities	1.01	1.22	1.33	0.93	0.97	1.15	0.98	0.71	0.96	0.61	0.70	0.75	0.59	0.85	1.19
Wholesale Trade	0.52	0.62	0.58	0.83	0.85	0.86	0.51	0.70	0.92	0.61	0.73	0.63	0.94	0.82	0.79
Retail Trade	0.83	0.84	0.84	1.12	1.04	0.96	0.97	0.97	0.95	0.83	0.95	0.97	1.05	1.03	1.01
Finance, Insurance, and Real Estate (FIRE)	1.00	0.97	0.93	0.77	0.97	1.14	0.87	1.03	0.91	0.60	0.67	0.74	0.93	1.17	1.08
Business/Professional Services	1.71	2.00	1.95	0.74	0.95	0.99	1.00	1.18	1.21	0.72	0.83	0.93	0.84	1.14	1.05
Nonprofit Services															
Health Services	0.61	0.71	0.69	1.01	0.87	0.77	0.82	0.87	0.77	0.80	0.79	0.78	0.87	1.04	1.13
Educational Services	1.60	1.27	1.34	0.30	0.43	0.44	0.57	0.68	0.67	0.33	0.46	0.67	0.76	0.85	0.83
Social Services/Organizations	1.77	1.44	1.55	0.90	0.85	0.96	0.92	0.76	0.89	0.58	0.77	0.85	0.98	0.90	0.88
Consumer Services	0.95	0.94	0.87	1.21	0.93	0.98	1.21	1.22	1.22	0.77	1.01	1.00	1.09	1.06	1.10
Government/Service															
Federal	7.18	5.49	6.10	2.55	1.63	1.23	1.94	1.42	1.61	2.98	2.68	2.78	3.10	2.71	2.36
Military	2.04	1.63	1.90	1.48	0.72	0.52	6.18	5.04	5.20	6.86	7.98	8.57	3.93	2.74	3.03
State and Local	0.94	0.71	0.70	2.06	1.89	1.91	0.90	0.85	0.93	0.81	0.79	0.91	0.87	0.97	0.96
Administration/Auxiliary	0.76	0.93	0.94	0.28	0.62	0.77	0.36	0.56	0.43	0.31	0.43	0.53	0.48	0.66	0.73

TABLE 4.8 (continued)

Location Quotients for Selected Industrial Categories, All Non-nodal Metros with Populations of More than 1 Million, 1974, 1990, and 1997

Resort/Retirement

Industrial Category	Riverside, CA			Tampa, FL			Fort Lauderdale, FL			Orlando, FL		
	1974	1990	1997	1974	1990	1997	1974	1990	1997	1974	1990	1997
Manufacturing	0.64	0.72	0.86	0.57	0.58	0.55	0.43	0.50	0.44	0.41	0.55	0.47
Transportation, Communications, and Utilities												
Transportation	0.46	0.97	1.28	0.89	0.68	0.74	0.87	0.84	1.11	1.05	1.00	1.13
Communications and Utilities	0.86	0.94	0.74	2.17	1.29	1.14	1.25	0.97	0.85	1.47	0.90	1.23
Wholesale Trade	0.67	0.77	0.90	1.10	1.06	1.02	0.74	1.15	1.29	1.20	1.04	1.01
Retail Trade	1.20	1.17	1.17	1.30	1.23	1.06	1.50	1.33	1.25	1.24	1.16	1.16
Finance, Insurance, and Real Estate (FIRE)	0.66	0.68	0.59	1.12	1.17	1.12	1.32	1.30	1.32	1.10	0.96	1.03
Business/Professional Services	0.68	0.77	0.71	1.28	1.48	2.00	1.32	1.38	1.30	1.18	1.22	1.22
Nonprofit Services												
Health Services	1.14	0.95	0.90	1.19	1.24	1.16	0.99	1.05	1.14	0.96	0.83	0.83
Educational Services	1.45	0.61	0.71	0.54	0.46	0.45	0.58	0.65	0.68	0.69	0.45	0.57
Social Services/Organizations	0.90	1.04	0.89	0.85	0.98	0.89	0.68	0.79	0.80	1.05	0.97	1.10
Consumer Services	1.37	1.20	1.22	1.43	1.26	1.09	2.18	1.54	1.28	1.96	2.72	2.75
Government/Service												
Federal	1.17	0.87	0.88	0.64	0.71	0.74	0.36	0.40	0.49	0.59	0.59	0.56
Military	2.46	1.65	1.33	0.70	0.66	0.64	0.29	0.30	0.35	1.60	1.37	0.58
State and Local	1.32	1.11	1.25	0.83	0.83	0.76	0.83	0.87	0.85	0.87	0.71	0.69
Administration/Auxiliary	0.21	0.59	0.71	0.55	0.70	0.76	0.33	0.61	0.69	0.51	1.36	1.51

Source: County Business Patterns.

San Diego among government/military metros and Fort Lauderdale and Tampa among resort/ retirement metros—are important centers within their regions. It is appropriate now to inquire regarding the extent to which these non-nodal metropolitan economies with populations of 1 million or more have become more specialized in corporate services or as diversified service centers. Table 4.8 presents 1974, 1990, and 1997 LQs for the principal industrial categories for the 13 metros with 1990 populations of more than 1 million that were classified as other than nodal.

The general finding from an examination of these measures is that specialization does not appear to have changed greatly for most of the 13 large metros shown. Among the *functional nodal* metros, Detroit, San Jose, and Rochester remain specialized in manufacturing, although Hartford is more heavily specialized in FIRE (largely insurance carriers and related banking activities). LQs for A/A are high for all these places except Hartford, which appears to have reduced its role as a host for insurance headquarters. Detroit and San Jose have attained high levels of specialization in business/professional services and A/A but are not well developed in financial services or transportation, communications, and utilities. Rochester remains structured essentially as it was in 1974.

As regards the large *government/service* metros, fast-growing Sacramento shows significant increases in LQs in FIRE, business/professional, transportation, and A/A, but only in FIRE has its LQ advanced to a level indicating significant specialization (1.14). The Washington metro remains very specialized in 1997 as the center of federal government activities, with an associated relatively high level of employment in business/professional services (e.g., lawyers, accountants, consultants, and engineers).

Among the three large metros classified as *government/military*, only San Diego and San Antonio have shown signs of developing increased specialization outside of federal and military employment. In San Diego, LQs rose sharply in business/professional services (from 1.00 to 1.21), and in San Antonio LQs rose in health services (from 0.87 to 1.13). The remaining large government/military metro, Norfolk, does not appear to have changed its specialization as measured in LQ terms.

The four large resort/retirement metros continued to show relatively high concentrations of employment in retailing and consumer services in 1997. Two of them, Fort Lauderdale and Tampa, maintained or improved their high 1974 LQs in FIRE and business/professional services. It seems clear that both of these metropolitan economies provide a fairly broad array of business and institutional services while functioning as resort/retirement centers. Their low LQs in A/A indicate that as yet they have not become major centers for corporate administrative offices, although these LQs did rise sharply during the period. Orlando has moved from a very low LQ in A/A (0.51) to become a relatively important location for administrative offices and headquarters (LQ of 1.51). It is also quite specialized in business/professional services (1.22), and of course in retailing (1.16) and consumer services (2.75). Riverside appears to have developed little service specialization.

Notes

1. Only one metro, Steubenville–Weirton, OH-WV, showed a net decline in employment during the 1974–97 period.

2. The appearance of manufacturing as a source of a small number of job increases in the manufacturing-oriented groups of metros—in spite of heavy *net* job decreases in most type/size groups—is explained by the fact that in some individual metros manufacturing employment did increase, although for the metro groups as a whole there was a net decline in manufacturing jobs.

3. In calling attention to how few jobs were created and how many jobs were lost in the manufacturing sector, no recognition is made of the fact that there were increases in productivity. The earnings measures presented in chapter 5 indicate that levels of earnings per worker in manufacturing were highest for the manufacturing-oriented groups, and that rates of increase in these earnings (1990–97) were somewhat higher than for other groups—presumably reflecting, in part, an increase in productivity.

4. It must also be recognized that, although these job-increase data capture the employment increase in activities classified as business/professional services, they do not and cannot capture the jobs that are being replaced. Here an example may be useful. If a manufacturer makes use of outside security guards and a public relations agent, instead of employing these people as in the past, employment in the category "business/professional services" increases, but the employment no longer shows up within the "manufacturing" category.

5. See M. Drennan, "The decline and rise of the New York economy," in M. Castells and J. Mollenkopf, eds., *Dual city: restructuring New York* (New York, NY: Russell Sage Foundation, 1991); J. Gottmann, "What are cities becoming the centers of?" in R. Knight and G. Gappert, eds., *Cities in a global society* (Newbury Park, CA: Sage, 1989); and S. Sassen, *The global city: New York, London, Tokyo* (Princeton, NJ: Princeton University Press, 1991).

6. Ann Markusen and Vicky Gwiasda, "Multi-polarity and the layering of functions in world cities: New York City's struggle to stay on top," *Journal of Urban and Regional Research* 18, 2: 167–93.

7. The evidence presented in chapter 6 on FIRE brokers and agents, banking, and business/professional services indicates high and rising relative earnings in the first two industrial categories but not the third. These findings are consistent with the above conclusion.

8. Fort Worth is not included in this list. Although ranked among the top third for growth, it is not specialized in FIRE categories or in business/professional services.

5

Transformations in Earnings
and in the Composition of Income

T wo additional transformations have occurred throughout the metropolitan system: changes in the earnings levels of workers in the various industrial categories, and changes in the composition of personal income.

Metropolitan Earnings Levels by Industrial Category

In examining workers' earnings at the industry level, we are examining another dimension of economic specialization. Earnings provide important clues to the extent of industrial specialization because they tend to reflect the average skill and training levels of workers involved in the various industries. Earnings levels may be influenced in some instances by the bargaining power of unions or even by foreign competition. Nevertheless, wage and salary levels in a given industry in a given place should provide a general indicator of the average level of the quality of labor relative to that of other industries within that metropolitan economy.

Measuring Relative Earnings Levels

The basic data examined were metro earnings in each industrial category, divided by the number of workers in the category. Both earnings and employment data are from *County Business Patterns*. The data were adjusted for variations among categories in hours worked.

Because there are no cost-of-living indexes available for most U.S. metropolitan areas, it is not possible to adjust for cost-of-living differences among metros. Therefore, a measure unaffected by price levels was used: An index of relative earnings ("earnings relative") was computed for each industrial category at the metro level. Earnings per worker (adjusted for weekly hours) in each industrial category were divided by earnings per worker (adjusted for weekly hours) in the eating-drinking industry (SIC 58). Earnings relatives were prepared for all metros with a population of 250,000 or more for the years 1974, 1990, and 1997.[1]

The rationale for using earnings per worker in eating-drinking as a *numeraire* is that this industry's production processes do not vary much from place to place and that it has a labor market that is competitive enough to assure that wage rates generally reflect differences in local costs of living. Accordingly, an earnings measure that compares earnings per worker in all other industries with eating-drinking should reflect relative levels of earnings in these industries, which in turn should provide an indicator of average levels of experience, skill, and training.

It is important to note that intermetropolitan differences among earnings relatives for a given industrial category may reflect differences in the makeup of the industrial category in one place or time from that in another. Thus the very high earnings relative of 5.05 for FIRE brokers and agents for the nodal metro group above 2 million population (see table 5.2 below) reflects the presence of a more specialized, well-paid investment community in many of these places, especially in New York, where the earnings relative for FIRE brokers and agents is 6.07.

Earnings Relatives and 1990–97 Changes

Examination of the measures for 1997 presented in table 5.1 shows that earnings relatives tend to vary, both among industries and (for given industries) among metros. This is readily seen by examining the 1997 range of metro-group earnings relatives along with median values for the several industry groups. Industries tend to fall into three categories on the basis of the medians of metro 1997 earnings relatives:

- *Highest:* manufacturing (2.52), communications-utilities (3.47), wholesaling (2.64), banking (2.82), insurance carriers (3.08), FIRE agents and brokers (2.69), health services (2.56), and federal government (3.27)
- *Middle:* construction (2.00), transportation (1.98), business-professional services (2.26), and state and local government (2.42)
- *Lowest:* retailing (1.41), educational services (1.80), social-membership services (1.25), and consumer services (1.50)

There were also significant *changes* in levels of earnings relatives during the period (see the 1990–97 medians of indexes of change in table 5.1), with some industries showing increases and others declines.

The manufacturing sector showed gains in levels of earnings relatives in both periods in virtually all type/size groups (table 5.2), even though employment in goods production was declining, with actual job losses in many metros. Gains in earnings relatives in the manufacturing sector likely reflect (at least partly) an upgrading of domestic manufacturing, as producers

TABLE 5.1
Earnings Relatives: Ranges and Medians, 1997; Medians of
Indexes of Change, 1990–1997, All Metros

Industrial Category	1997 Range of Group Averages	1997 Median	1990–97 Median of Indexes of Change[a]
Construction	1.74–2.32	2.00	0.95
Manufacturing	1.99–3.26	2.52	1.03
Transportation, Communications, and Utilities			
Transportation	1.62–2.11	1.98	0.94
Communications and Utilities	2.93–3.70	3.47	1.09
Wholesale Trade	2.20–3.30	2.64	1.04
Retail Trade	1.36–1.43	1.41	0.98
Finance, Insurance, Real Estate (FIRE)			
Banking/Credit Agencies	2.32–3.70	2.82	1.16
Insurance Carriers	2.22–3.39	3.08	1.13
FIRE Agents and Brokers	2.32–5.05	2.69	1.19
Business/Professional Services	1.86–2.70	2.26	1.05
Nonprofit Services			
Health Services	2.36–2.67	2.56	1.06
Educational Services	1.56–2.03	1.80	1.04
Social Services/Organizations	1.12–1.32	1.25	1.03
Consumer Services	1.40–1.73	1.50	1.03
Government/Service			
Federal	3.02–3.88	3.27	1.13
Military	1.01–2.33	1.30	1.04
State and Local	2.23–2.63	2.42	1.01

Notes: Earnings relatives were calculated as follows. Hours-adjusted earnings per worker in each industry were divided by hours-adjusted earnings per worker in Eating-Drinking places. The measures shown were calculated on the basis of totals for type/size metro groups.

a. Indexes of change were calculated by dividing the 1997 earnings relative by the 1990 earnings relative for each type/size metro group.

Source: County Business Patterns.

who employed lower-wage, less-skilled workers faced heavy competition from foreign-based plants and as more productive existing plants gave rise to higher workers' earnings.

Still another observation is that the relative level of construction workers' earnings declined in virtually every metro group. Presumably, this was at least partly due to the declining ability of labor unions to influence wage patterns in this industry.

TABLE 5.2
Earnings Relatives, 1997; Earnings Relatives' Indexes of Change, 1990/1974 and 1997/1990; and Location Quotients (LQ), 1997 by Type/Size of Metro Group

Industrial Category	NODAL > 2 MILLION Earnings Relative				NODAL 1-2 MILLION Earnings Relative				NODAL 250,000–1 MILLION Earnings Relative			
	1997	Change, 1990/1974	Change, 1997/1990	LQ 1997	1997	Change, 1990/1974	Change, 1997/1990	LQ 1997	1997	Change, 1990/1974	Change, 1997/1990	LQ 1997
Construction	2.03	0.81	0.94	0.91	2.00	0.78	0.95	1.02	1.95	0.80	0.95	1.06
Manufacturing	2.40	1.05	1.03	0.85	2.52	1.03	1.05	0.93	2.58	1.07	1.00	0.90
Transportation, Communications, and Utilities												
Transportation	1.95	0.90	0.94	1.21	2.01	0.90	0.89	1.40	2.04	0.98	0.87	1.14
Communications and Utilities	3.44	1.62	1.13	1.10	3.47	1.67	1.13	1.19	3.70	2.02	1.19	1.05
Wholesale Trade	2.66	1.00	1.04	1.23	2.64	0.97	1.04	1.28	2.72	1.00	1.03	1.14
Retail Trade	1.40	0.96	0.99	0.89	1.43	0.94	0.99	0.97	1.41	0.92	0.97	1.03
Finance, Insurance, and Real Estate (FIRE)												
Banking/Credit Agencies	3.70	1.23	1.32	1.20	3.03	1.12	1.28	1.18	2.95	1.24	1.16	1.20
Insurance Carriers	3.17	1.14	1.19	1.23	3.10	1.16	1.14	1.42	3.12	1.16	1.13	1.67
FIRE Agents and Brokers	5.05	1.33	1.38	1.51	3.28	1.23	1.22	1.18	3.99	1.30	1.42	1.00
Business/Professional Services	2.49	1.15	1.06	1.35	2.42	1.12	1.08	1.17	2.22	1.11	1.04	1.01
Nonprofit Services												
Health Services	2.40	1.18	1.06	0.99	2.41	1.20	1.04	0.93	2.59	1.22	1.07	1.03
Educational Services	1.86	0.88	1.08	1.41	1.67	0.89	1.01	0.87	1.64	0.77	1.01	0.93
Social Services/Organizations	1.32	0.93	1.03	0.99	1.25	0.94	1.03	0.96	1.21	0.93	1.03	1.08
Consumer Services	1.73	0.97	1.04	1.05	1.53	0.96	1.06	0.97	1.50	0.97	1.04	0.90
Government/Service												
Federal	3.02	0.88	1.15	0.83	3.22	0.89	1.13	0.87	3.27	0.92	1.09	0.92
Military	1.02	0.96	0.97	0.44	1.01	0.89	0.95	0.46	1.63	1.02	1.04	0.99
State and Local	2.42	1.02	1.01	0.82	2.34	1.01	1.02	0.83	2.35	1.04	0.99	0.87

TABLE 5.2 (continued)

Industrial Category	FUNCTIONAL NODAL > 250,000 Earnings Relative				MANUFACTURING/SERVICES > 250,000 Earnings Relative				MANUFACTURING > 250,000 Earnings Relative			
	1997	Change, 1990/1974	Change, 1997/1990	LQ 1997	1997	Change, 1990/1974	Change, 1997/1990	LQ 1997	1997	Change, 1990/1974	Change, 1997/1990	LQ 1997
Construction	2.26	0.78	0.97	0.95	2.17	0.78	0.99	0.81	2.32	0.78	0.95	1.07
Manufacturing	3.26	1.05	1.10	1.45	2.75	1.08	1.08	1.22	2.85	1.03	1.01	1.55
Transportation, Communications, and Utilities												
Transportation	2.11	0.93	0.94	0.90	1.98	0.97	0.98	0.73	2.11	0.84	0.98	0.82
Communications and Utilities	3.58	2.30	1.04	0.85	3.43	1.82	1.07	0.85	3.62	1.95	1.03	0.85
Wholesale Trade	3.30	1.00	1.12	1.06	2.52	1.01	1.04	0.76	2.64	0.93	1.00	0.99
Retail Trade	1.42	0.91	0.97	0.96	1.38	0.92	1.00	1.03	1.41	0.89	0.98	1.09
Finance, Insurance, and Real Estate (FIRE)												
Banking/Credit Agencies	2.82	1.10	1.16	0.97	2.46	1.09	1.07	0.78	2.53	1.12	1.09	0.82
Insurance Carriers	3.39	1.08	1.14	1.37	3.07	1.05	1.19	1.12	3.08	1.04	1.09	0.72
FIRE Agents and Brokers	3.41	1.20	1.26	0.85	2.61	1.16	1.09	0.64	2.57	1.18	1.00	0.57
Business/Professional Services	2.70	1.08	1.11	1.10	2.26	1.19	1.05	0.76	2.08	1.00	1.05	0.71
Nonprofit Services												
Health Services	2.66	1.17	1.06	0.97	2.66	1.21	1.10	1.30	2.67	1.15	1.06	1.04
Educational Services	1.95	0.89	1.04	1.08	2.03	0.83	1.01	1.68	1.65	0.69	1.11	0.80
Social Services/Organizations	1.25	0.92	1.03	0.93	1.25	1.00	0.98	1.03	1.19	0.94	1.02	1.03
Consumer Services	1.53	0.93	1.02	0.78	1.42	0.90	1.02	0.78	1.54	NA	1.05	0.96
Government/Service												
Federal	3.48	0.89	1.17	0.64	3.39	0.91	1.12	0.79	3.08	0.91	1.07	0.58
Military	1.14	1.03	0.98	0.42	1.30	0.99	1.20	0.68	1.24	1.13	1.06	0.56
State and Local	2.63	1.01	1.03	0.79	2.57	1.04	1.06	1.10	2.55	1.02	1.01	0.82

TABLE 5.2 (continued)

Industrial Category	GOVERNMENT/SERVICE > 250,000 Earnings Relative				GOVERNMENT/MILITARY > 250,000 Earnings Relative				RESORT/RETIREMENT > 250,000 Earnings Relative			
	1997	Change, 1990/1974	Change, 1997/1990	LQ 1997	1997	Change, 1990/1974	Change, 1997/1990	LQ 1997	1997	Change, 1990/1974	Change, 1997/1990	LQ 1997
Construction	1.90	0.83	0.91	1.10	1.84	0.88	0.94	1.08	1.74	0.76	1.00	1.31
Manufacturing	2.49	1.05	1.04	0.61	2.19	1.15	0.95	0.63	1.99	1.00	0.98	0.54
Transportation, Communications, and Utilities												
Transportation	1.88	1.10	0.92	0.73	1.80	1.19	0.90	0.74	1.62	0.98	0.94	0.94
Communications and Utilities	3.56	1.95	1.15	1.07	3.24	2.01	1.03	0.88	2.93	2.23	1.09	0.92
Wholesale Trade	2.54	1.00	1.04	0.81	2.47	1.04	1.08	0.76	2.20	0.95	1.07	0.90
Retail Trade	1.40	0.94	0.98	0.98	1.38	0.93	0.98	0.99	1.36	0.92	1.02	1.15
Finance, Insurance, and Real Estate (FIRE)												
Banking/Credit Agencies	2.82	1.12	1.21	0.83	2.47	1.15	1.08	0.84	2.32	1.05	1.19	0.91
Insurance Carriers	2.81	1.10	1.11	1.11	2.76	1.13	1.02	0.75	2.62	1.02	1.09	0.64
FIRE Agents and Brokers	2.69	1.25	1.12	0.91	2.59	1.18	1.19	0.81	2.32	1.15	1.16	1.21
Business/Professional Services	2.66	1.08	1.07	1.22	2.19	1.07	0.91	0.95	1.86	0.92	1.00	1.27
Nonprofit Services												
Health Services	2.54	1.32	1.05	0.93	2.56	1.37	1.03	0.94	2.36	1.11	1.04	1.00
Educational Services	1.80	0.96	0.99	1.10	1.63	0.93	1.05	0.72	1.56	0.79	1.06	0.57
Social Services/Organizations	1.62	0.92	1.05	1.17	1.19	0.93	1.05	0.94	1.12	0.96	1.05	0.87
Consumer Services	1.43	0.99	1.03	0.89	1.40	1.01	1.03	1.05	1.57	0.99	1.04	2.09
Government/Service												
Federal	3.88	0.92	1.19	2.31	3.11	0.99	1.10	2.10	3.05	0.88	1.17	0.67
Military	2.28	0.95	1.22	1.18	2.33	0.90	1.06	5.85	1.47	0.87	0.98	0.73
State and Local	2.44	1.04	0.99	1.24	2.53	1.10	0.98	0.99	2.23	1.01	1.03	0.88

Note: Earnings relatives were calculated as follows: Hours-adjusted earnings per worker in each industry were divided by hours-adjusted earnings per worker in Eating-Drinking places.

NA = not available

Source: County Business Patterns.

Comparisons of Earnings Relatives and Related Measures

To facilitate analysis, table 5.2 presents information on 1997 earnings relatives, indexes of change (1974–90 and 1990–97) in earnings relatives, and 1997 location quotients for selected industry categories for metro groups.

Nodal Metros

Table 5.2 shows (as discussed in chapter 2) that the largest nodal groups tend to have relatively high concentrations of employment (high group LQs) in these categories: transportation, wholesaling, banking, insurance carriers, FIRE agents and brokers, and business/professional services. The new finding is that in two of these five categories—banking and FIRE agents and brokers—the largest nodal groups lead once again in virtually every comparison of earnings relatives and of rates of increase in earnings levels, as indicated by indexes of change.

This was especially the case among the very largest metros, the nodal places with 2 million or more population. As a group, these metros—which were already quite large in 1974, and which for the most part were established as major centers of business and corporate services—increased the relative levels of their wage and salary rates sharply in these industries. This suggests that, in these areas, they were moving to higher levels of specialization in the sense of attaining higher levels of skill and expertise.

New York Relative to Other Large Nodal Metros

In light of the discussion in chapter 4 about New York as a world city, it should be useful to compare earnings relatives in New York and other large nodal cities for the industrial classifications that cover financial and business services. The earnings relatives for 1997 and indexes of 1990–97 changes in earnings relatives in these service categories should provide some evidence for the extent of specialization, as reflected in average levels of skill and training of personnel.

Table 5.3 presents—for a selected list of large nodal metros (i.e., New York and those discussed in chapter 4 as the most likely competitors of New York)—earnings relatives and indexes of 1990–97 changes in relatives in the three service categories most clearly involved in New York's performance as a world city: banking, FIRE agents and brokers, and business/professional services.

New York shows the highest levels of earnings in banking and in FIRE agents and brokers, but ranks lower in business/professional services. Moreover, New York made the greatest (percentage) gains in earnings levels in banking and FIRE agents and brokers, but again not in business/professional services. If we look back at the analysis in chapter 4, we find that New York outranked all large nodal metros in LQs for banking and FIRE agents and brokers, but not in business/professional services (see table 4.7). Taken together, these findings indicate New

TABLE 5.3

Earnings Relatives, 1997, and Indexes of Change, 1990–97, for Three Industrial Categories in Selected Large Nodal Metros

Metro	1997 Earnings Relatives[a]			Indexes of Change in Earnings Relatives, 1990–1997[a]		
	Banking	FIRE Agents and Brokers	Business/ Professional Services	Banking	FIRE Agents and Brokers	Business/ Professional Services
Los Angeles	2.97 (8)	3.47 (6)	2.30 (10)	1.40 (4)	1.29 (5)	1.07 (6)
New York	5.12 (1)	6.74 (1)	2.26 (11)	1.67 (1)	1.55 (1)	1.12 (5)
Chicago	3.42 (3)	3.88 (4)	2.46 (7)	1.10 (11)	1.13 (9–10)	1.00 (10–11)
Philadelphia	2.78 (10)	3.50 (5)	2.76 (4)	1.18 (8)	1.22 (6)	1.13 (3)
Boston	3.34 (4)	4.32 (3)	2.85 (3)	1.44 (3)	1.39 (3)	1.13 (4)
Houston	2.64 (11)	3.38 (8)	2.47 (6)	1.05 (12)	1.36 (4)	1.05 (7)
Atlanta	3.10 (5)	3.40 (7)	2.41 (8)	1.14 (10)	1.13 (9–10)	1.03 (8–9)
Dallas	3.13 (6)	2.88 (10)	2.35 (9)	1.37 (5)	1.21 (7)	1.00 (10–11)
Anaheim	3.05 (7)	2.95 (9)	2.49 (5)	1.27 (6)	1.11 (12)	1.03 (8–9)
Phoenix	2.60 (12)	2.63 (13)	1.92 (12)	1.15 (9)	1.09 (13)	0.91 (12)
Seattle	2.84 (9)	2.68 (11)	2.94 (1–2)	1.26 (7)	1.17 (8)	1.41 (1)
San Francisco	4.08 (2)	4.39 (2)	2.94 (1–2)	1.66 (2)	1.52 (2)	1.28 (2)
Fort Worth	2.30 (13)	2.66 (12)	1.78 (13)	1.01 (13)	1.12 (11)	0.90 (13)

Notes: a. Rankings are shown in parentheses.

Source: County Business Patterns.

York's greater strength vis-à-vis the rest of the metropolitan system in financial and investment sectors than in its other producer services; they also provide evidence that New York has strengthened its specialization at a faster pace in recent years than have the other large nodal metros. Moreover, San Francisco, New York's closest rival in LQs for banking and FIRE agents and brokers (see table 4.7), is also its closest rival in comparable earnings relatives and indexes of change (see table 5.3).

Functional Nodal Metros

For functional nodal metros (with populations of more than 250,000),[2] earnings relatives are particularly revealing (see table 5.2). Not only do these metros show the highest relatives for manufacturing, matching very high employment concentrations (LQ of 1.45), but they rank among the top three or four metro groups in earnings relatives for transportation, wholesaling, banking, FIRE agents and brokers, business/professional services, health, educational services, and state and local government services. These command-center metros are not characterized by large shares of employment in these industrial categories, and it is not clear why many of them have developed this relatively high wage structure. The analysis of earnings and income given below will confirm, however, that a large number of these places have fared well.

Manufacturing/Service Metros

Manufacturing/service metros (with populations of more than 250,000), like functional nodal places, are characterized by high earnings relatives and high LQs in manufacturing. In addition, both average relatives and employment LQs rank at or above the middle among the various type/size groups in health services, educational services, and state and local government— which is consistent with the observation made above that many of these places are old manufacturing centers that have developed as educational and service centers.

Manufacturing Metros

The manufacturing group of metros (with populations of more than 250,000) ranks high in both average earnings relatives and average LQs for the large manufacturing industrial sector. In the health services sector, the group earnings relative is approximately the same as for the manufacturing/service group, and the LQ is well below the comparable value for that group.

Government/Service Metros

Government/service metros (with populations of more than 250,000), many of which are fast-growing, dynamic economies, are characterized by largely medium or low earnings relatives across the whole range of industry categories, with the exception of business/professional services, where relatives of 2.66 ranked second among metro groups.

Government/Military Metros

Government/military metros (with populations of more than 250,000) are characterized by relatively heavy concentrations of employment in the military and the federal government (LQs of 5.85 and 2.10). This group's earnings relatives were relatively low in all industrial categories except the military and state and local government.

Resort/Retirement Metros

The remarkable finding for resort/retirement metros (with populations of more than 250,000) is that their earnings relatives rank at or near the bottom when compared with all other metro groups, except for consumer services, whose relative (1.57) ranks near the middle. (The LQ of 2.09 for consumer services indicates very high employment specialization.)

Just why earnings relatives tend to be so low among resort/retirement places is not clear. One possible explanation is that, because many of them have largely consumer-oriented economies, they have an unusually high demand for retail and other services requiring low-skilled labor. Under such conditions, the wages of unskilled workers may be bid up to such an extent that the difference between earnings of unskilled and skilled employees is significantly reduced. It may be objected that market forces should restore the differential between unskilled and skilled workers. Yet it is not unreasonable that, in such fast-growing economies, *relatively* high earnings for low-skilled workers may persist, given that costs of travel and resettlement pose greater barriers to migration for such workers than for those with higher skills and earnings levels.

The Transformation in the Composition of Earnings

The above analysis has shown significant changes in earnings relatives of industries over time, as well as significant differences in earnings relatives among groups of metros when compared by industrial category. The conclusion to be drawn from these findings must be that the very dramatic shifts from goods to service *employment* examined in chapter 4 contributed to changes in the industrial composition of workers' earnings. For example, we observed in chapter 4 that shares of job increases accounted for by health services were an important source of employment growth, whereas in table 5.1 we observed that health services were characterized by increases in earnings relatives.

Thus, the dramatic shifts among certain major industries in shares of total employment, together with the variation in earnings levels among these industries, have worked together to bring about a substantial transformation in the composition of earnings. The data tell us nothing, of course, about the shifts in the employment of women or about the shift from blue- to white-collar employment. Further analysis would be needed to break down the transformation in earnings levels among various groups of workers within the several type/size groups of metros.

Changes in the Composition of Personal Income

We now turn from analyzing relative levels of workers' earnings among industries to examining and comparing the three components of personal income: workers' earnings (all industries combined); transfer payments; and dividends, interest, and rent payments.[3]

Adjusting the Data

In comparing the BEA dollar-value estimates of earnings, TP, and DIR for 1997 with those for 1974, it was necessary to adjust for inflation during the period. A single deflator, the CPI, was used to adjust for inflation because price indexes for individual metros were available for only a limited number of places. Deflators were not available to adjust for differences in cost of living among metros but, for three reasons, the analysis should not be compromised.

First, cost-of-living differences among metros in a given year are not an important consideration when examining rates of change in levels of earned and non-earned income of individual metros for a period of years. Second, comparisons among metros of the distribution of personal income between earnings, TP, and DIR in a given year do not require adjustment for cost-of-living differences among metros.

Third, it is not apparent that cost-of-living adjustments are appropriate for non-earned income payments. For example, it is not clear that the high levels of DIR per capita found among the Florida resorts are in any way dependent on local costs of living and should be deflated in recognition of such costs. In large measure, the same could be said regarding Social Security retirement benefits.

Earnings (All Industries Combined)

Two measures of workers' earnings are examined: earnings per worker and earnings per capita (table 5.4). The latter measure is presented simply to make it possible to compare earnings with TP and DIR on a per capita basis.

Earnings per Worker

Earnings per worker for 1997 show sizable differences among size categories of metros, with levels significantly lower for the metro groups with less than 250,000 population than for the comparable groups with larger populations (thus the smallest nodal size group has lower earnings per worker than the next larger size group of nodal places, etc.) (see table 5.4).

TABLE 5.4

Measures of Earned and Non-earned Income by Type/Size of Metro Group, 1997 (in 1997 dollars)

Metro Type/Size Group		Earnings per Worker	Rank	Earnings per Capita	Rank	Income per Capita	Rank	TP per Capita[a]	Rank	DIR per Capita[b]	Rank
Nodal	> 2 Million	33,631	1	20,478	1	29,956	1	4,341	4	5,137	3
Nodal	1–2 Million	30,771	3	20,217	2	29,177	2	3,836	12	5,124	4
Nodal	250,000–1 Million	29,075	4	18,715	4	27,199	4	3,985	9	4,499	6
Nodal	< 250,000	24,120	11	15,119	8	22,815	10	3,770	13	3,926	10
Functional Nodal	> 250,000	31,765	2	19,092	3	27,708	3	4,056	8	4,560	5
Manufacturing/Service	> 250,000	28,397	7	16,035	7	24,770	8	4,672	2	4,063	8
Manufacturing/Service	< 250,000	23,905	13	13,951	13	21,532	13	4,088	6	3,493	13
Manufacturing	> 250,000	28,778	5	16,109	6	23,745	9	3,903	11	3,734	11
Government/Service	> 250,000	28,681	6	17,308	5	25,524	6	3,981	10	4,235	7
Government/Service	< 250,000	23,938	12	14,965	10	22,598	11	3,610	14	4,023	9
Government/Military	> 250,000	26,065	9	14,635	11	22,334	12	4,085	7	3,614	12
Government/Military	< 250,000	22,100	14	12,236	14	19,413	14	4,297	5	2,880	14
Resort/Retirement	> 250,000	28,382	8	14,992	9	25,139	7	4,431	3	5,716	2
Resort/Retirement	< 250,000	24,343	10	14,039	12	25,598	5	4,779	1	6,780	1
Total, United States		28,735		16,787		25,288		4,147		4,354	

Notes: a. TP is Transfer Payments.

b. DIR is Dividends, Interest, and Rent Payments.

Source: U.S. Bureau of Economic Analysis.

When rates of change in earnings per worker are examined for the two subperiods 1974–90 and 1990–97 (table 5.5), we observe that during the earlier period earnings declined in virtually all size/type metro groups. During the 1990s, however, earnings levels increased in most groups, rising for the United States as a whole from an annual rate of –0.04 (1974–90) to 0.30 (1990–97).

The declining earnings levels of the earlier period are generally associated with declining worker productivity in the U.S. economy. The 1990s (as noted in chapter 1) brought improvements in productivity within the U.S. economy. Such improvements, however, do not appear to have raised the overall level of real wages for some metro groups by the late 1990s. The nodal groups (other than those with less than 250,000 population), along with the larger functional nodal places, appear to have turned in the best performance, whereas the remaining groups have done less well.

Earnings per Capita

Earnings per capita are of course smaller than earnings per worker. But the group rankings of earnings per capita are similar for the most part to the group rankings of earnings per worker (see table 5.4).

When group growth rates in earnings per capita (1974–90 and 1990–97) are compared with group growth rates of earnings per worker, they are higher in every comparison (see table 5.5). This more favorable performance of the growth measures for earnings per capita is due to gains everywhere in the shares of the population employed (i.e., in the ratios of employment to population, or E/P ratios). During the period, women entered the workforce in increasing numbers, the oversized baby boom generation entered the job market, and the rate of unemployment declined.

Non-Earned Income

The rapid increase in the level of receipts of non-earned income must surely be regarded as one of the most significant developments of the U.S. economy during the period 1974–97. Dividends, interest, and rent payments per capita increased at an annual rate of 2.34 percent for the United States as a whole (see table 5.5), with DIR rising from 13.8 to 17.2 percent of total U.S. personal income (see table 1.8). Transfer payments per capita increased from 1974 to 1997 at an annual rate of 2.6 percent (see table 5.5), bringing TP from 12.5 to 16.4 percent of total U.S. personal income (see table 1.8). In contrast, earnings per capita rose at an *annual rate* of only 0.92 percent (see table 5.5), declining from 73.6 to 66.4 percent of total U.S. personal income.

TABLE 5.5

Rates of Growth: Earnings per Worker, Earnings per Capita, Income per Capita, TP per Capita, and DIR per Capita, by Type/Size of Metro Group, 1974–97 and 1990–97

| | Rate of Growth | | | | | | | | | |
| Metro Type/Size Group | Earnings per Worker | | Earnings per Capita | | Income per Capita | | TP per Capita[a] | | DIR per Capita[b] | |
	1974–97	1990–97	1974–97	1990–97	1974–97	1990–97	1974–97	1990–97	1974–97	1990–97
Nodal > 2 Million	0.28	0.63	1.21	0.90	1.51	0.98	2.24	3.08	2.19	-0.26
Nodal 1–2 Million	0.07	0.70	1.21	1.45	1.53	1.33	2.49	2.67	2.25	-0.05
Nodal 250,000–1 Million	0.14	0.50	1.30	1.51	1.71	1.53	2.86	3.15	2.72	0.33
Nodal < 250,000	-0.49	0.11	0.59	1.44	1.29	1.38	2.93	2.98	2.36	-0.19
Functional Nodal > 250,000	-0.08	0.63	1.00	1.25	1.45	1.22	2.68	2.64	2.61	-0.02
Manufacturing/Service > 250,000	-0.04	0.02	0.86	0.59	1.38	0.85	2.79	3.26	2.33	-0.58
Manufacturing/Service < 250,000	-0.41	-0.11	0.68	1.00	1.28	1.16	2.83	3.05	2.54	-0.22
Manufacturing > 250,000	-0.22	0.14	0.65	1.00	1.21	1.05	2.91	2.58	2.51	-0.14
Government/Service > 250,000	-0.12	0.10	0.90	0.60	1.31	0.76	2.26	2.63	2.43	-0.18
Government/Service < 250,000	-0.25	0.03	0.94	1.11	1.42	1.28	2.54	2.95	2.55	0.52
Government/Military > 250,000	0.00	0.08	0.73	0.47	1.24	0.78	2.44	2.73	2.37	0.02
Government/Military < 250,000	-0.47	-0.21	0.10	0.63	0.91	1.15	3.15	3.42	2.31	0.32
Resort/Retirement > 250,000	-0.06	-0.27	0.85	0.42	1.24	0.38	2.00	2.58	1.78	-1.17
Resort/Retirement < 250,000	-0.24	-0.12	0.73	0.64	1.53	0.79	2.56	2.87	2.93	-0.19
Total, United States	-0.04	0.30	0.92	0.95	1.37	1.04	2.57	2.94	2.34	-0.25

Notes: a. TP is Transfer Payments.
b. DIR is Dividends, Interest, and Rent Payments.

Source: U.S. Bureau of Economic Analysis.

Dividends, Interest, and Rent

The overall increase in DIR as a share of income (see table 1.8) must be regarded as evidence of rising inequality in the distribution of income among families and individuals. Although a rise in DIR spread evenly as a proportion of everyone's personal income would not of itself alter the distribution of income, such proportionality is clearly not the case. DIR is derived from income-yielding assets, and such assets are known to be distributed disproportionately among wealthy people.[4]

Moreover, there is clear evidence that some metros have gained more from the increases in DIR payments than have others. The *gains* in average DIR per capita range widely—from $1,177 (1997 dollars) for residents of government/military metros (with less than 250,000 population) to $3,289 for residents of smaller resort/retirement metros (not shown in table).

Table 5.4 makes clear the extent to which resort/retirement places have benefited from DIR, presumably because retirees and well-to-do persons have elected to emigrate to these locales and have brought their portfolios with them. On average, residents of the two resort/retirement type/size groups receive far and away the largest DIR of any group—accounting for income flows of 22.7 and 26.5 percent of total personal income in the two groups (see table 1.8).

Among the groups of metros, levels of 1997 DIR ranged widely: from $6,780 for the smallest resort/retirement group to $2,880 for the smaller-size government/military group (see table 5.4).

Such differences in income from investments and property represent very real differences in the level and distribution of wealth, and we are likely to find their proxies in other aspects of metropolitan life—in the presence or absence of cultural institutions, in recreational and government facilities, and in the size of the tax base upon which government-financed infrastructure is founded.

Transfer Payments

Although smaller than DIR, transfer payments accounted for more than 16 percent of total personal income in the U.S. economy in 1997 (see table 1.8). Moreover, shares increased substantially in every type/size group of metros during the 1974–97 period.

To better analyze the role of TP, a major component, retirement/disability payments (largely Social Security retirement payments), hereafter "R-D payments," was examined separately (table 5.6). An intriguing observation is that the level of these payments is relatively high in several type/size groups that are quite different in economic specialization. For example, R-D payments are more than 14 percent of the level of workers' earnings not only in the resort/retirement metros (both size groups), but also in the smallest-size (less than 250,000 population) manufacturing/service group and in both government/military groups.

TABLE 5.6
Retirement/Disability (RD) Payments Calculated as Percentages of Worker Earnings, 1997;
Metros Ranked Highest (Top Third) for RD Payments in 1997 and Analyzed by 1974–97 Employment Growth, by Type/Size of Metro Group

Metro Type/Size Group		1997 Retirement/Disability (R/D) Payments as Percentage of Earnings	Number of Metros	Number of Metros Ranked in Top Third for R/D Payments as Percentage of Earnings	Number of Metros Ranked in Top Third That Are Ranked High, Middle, Low for Employment Growth		
					High	Middle	Low
Nodal	> 2 Million	8.9	16	1	—	—	1
Nodal	1–2 Million	9.5	18	0	—	—	—
Nodal	250,000–1 Million	10.6	22	5	—	2	3
Nodal	< 250,000	12.3	32	4	1	1	2
Functional Nodal	> 250,000	10.4	17	1	—	—	1
Manufacturing/Service	> 250,000	13.2	12	3	—	1	2
Manufacturing/Service	< 250,000	14.2	44	25	—	7	18
Manufacturing	> 250,000	12.2	22	5	—	1	4
Government/Service	> 250,000	11.8	33	8	2	3	3
Government/Service	< 250,000	12.1	29	8	3	1	4
Government/Military	> 250,000	14.7	16	10	2	7	1
Government/Military	< 250,000	18.0	21	17	4	6	7
Resort/Retirement	> 250,000	15.1	13	7	6	1	—
Resort/Retirement	< 250,000	18.0	12	8	7	—	1

Source: U.S. Bureau of Economic Analysis.

To shed light on why high levels of R-D payments occur in such dissimilar groups of metros, the level of these payments was compared with rates of employment growth. R-D payments were related to earnings (i.e., expressed as a percentage of earnings) for each metro, the percentages were arrayed, and the array was divided into three equal groups: high, middle, and low.[5] Metros were then similarly ranked for rate of growth in total employment and classified as high, middle, and low.

Table 5.6 shows the number of metros in each type/size group that are classified as high in their *R-D payments relative to earnings* (1997). Alongside these are shown the number of these metros classified as high, low, or medium in rate of employment growth.

Paradoxically, the manufacturing/service places that were classified as high in R-D payments were predominantly low-growth places, whereas the resort/retirement places that were classified as high in R-D were predominantly high-growth places. The explanation for this situation appears to be that, among the small manufacturing/service metros, employment has been hard-hit, resulting in low savings and frequently preventing elderly people from migrating to sunny retirement communities. In such places, retirees are less likely to move far from home, and metro retirement payments are likely to be high in relation to current workers' earnings.

Conversely, for high-growth resort/retirement metros, the explanation appears to be quite different. These places—located largely in California and Florida—are popular havens for the elderly. These places' high retirement benefits are consistent with high in-migration of retirees and a high rate of employment growth. The result is that retirement payments (i.e., Social Security) are high in relation to earnings.

This resort/retirement scenario also appears to apply to other metro groups. For example, in addition to the resort/retirement places, 12 metros in other groups were classified as high for both R-D benefits and employment growth (see table 5.6). All of these places are located in the South or West, and presumably would have been likely target areas for retiree migration:

Nodal
Ocala, FL

Government/service
Olympia, WA
Las Cruces, NM
Salem, OR
San Luis Obispo, CA
Tucson, AZ

Government/military
Bremerton, WA
Colorado Springs, CO
Fort Walton Beach, FL

Government/military (continued)
Huntsville, AL
Panama City, FL
Yuma, AR

Finally, it is clear that a majority of government/military places depend heavily on retirement transfer payments. Sixty-two percent (10 out of 16) of these metros with 250,000 or more population and 81 percent (17 out of 21) with less than 250,000 population are ranked among the top third of the R-D percentage of the earnings array. Accordingly, a large majority of government/military places appear to be favored as retirement centers.

Just why this is so would appear to have no single explanation. As we have seen, six of these metros are high-growth places that probably qualify as attractive retirement centers for the reasons discussed above. But others also seem to qualify in climate and location, even though they are less well known as retirement centers and have grown less rapidly. In addition, the large majority of government/military places are located in the South and West, where frequently—though not always—there are decided cost-of-living advantages. For a sizable group of retirees that have had military careers, these places offer low-cost medical services at military hospitals and opportunities to shop at military exchanges at below-market prices, along with generally low cost-of-living characteristics.

Employment/Population Ratios

In general, one might assume that a high ratio of employment to population (E/P) in a metro indicates a high level of robustness—a high level in the demand for labor. There is certainly some persuasive evidence that this is the case. For example, among the 3 largest nodal groups (250,000 or more population), the 10 metros whose E/P ratios ranked highest in 1997 form a list of places generally regarded as economically vigorous:

San Francisco, CA	80.0
Des Moines, IA	75.9
Omaha, NE	73.3
Seattle, WA	72.8
Minneapolis–Saint Paul, MN	72.5
Dallas, TX	71.9
Nashville, TN	71.7
Denver, CO	71.5
Fort Wayne, IN	70.3
Portland, OR	70.2

Conversely, metros with the lowest E/P ratios are usually regarded as distressed, including such old manufacturing places as Gary–Hammond, IN; Hamilton–Middletown, OH; New Bedford–Fall River, MA; and Youngstown–Warren, OH. There were, however, also retirement centers, such as Daytona Beach, Fort Lauderdale, Fort Myers, and Lakeland–Winter Haven (all in Florida), whose E/P ratios are low but which showed little evidence of distress in view of the high levels of non-earned income and of total income per capita. Accordingly, E/P ratios and changes in these ratios are measures to be considered, but they must be examined along with other criteria in determining how metros or groups of metros have fared.

Comparing Measures of Earnings and Income Change: A Summary

Table 5.7 brings together—for each type/size group of metros—measures for 1997 employment/population ratios; 1974–97 employment rates of change; and both 1997 levels and 1974–97 rates of change in earnings, non-earned income, and total personal income. Table 5.8 presents the same measures for the most recent period, 1990–97. All measures were based on metro rankings. First, each metro was classified according to whether it ranked within the highest, middle, or lowest third of the entire array. Second, for each group of metros, the percentage of places in the highest, middle, and lowest categories was calculated. In the discussion that follows, all references to these measures are to table 5.7, unless table 5.8 is specified.

Nodal Metros

The very large nodal metros, those with 2 million or more population, clearly lead the entire metropolitan system in income per capita. Although it may be argued that the high level of 1997 earnings per worker among all these metropolitan economies may partly reflect a higher cost of living than elsewhere, it must also be noted that 69 percent of these metros ranked in the highest category for 1974–97 growth in earnings per worker. Three-fourths of these places also rank in the top third among all metros for comparisons of 1997 DIR per capita. A much smaller percentage (38 percent), however, falls in the top third of the array for TP per capita.

Yet there was considerable variation among these metros in rates of employment growth. During the most recent period (1990–97), of the 16 metros in the nodal population group of 2 million and above, only 4 (25 percent) (Atlanta, Dallas, Houston, and Phoenix) were among the fastest-growing third of all metros, whereas 11 (69 percent) were in the slowest-growing third (see table 5.8).

The findings for the nodal metros with 1 million to 2 million population are similar, although the number of places ranked in the top third for E/P ratios in 1997 was much higher (72 percent) and for income per capita and DIR per capita somewhat lower (but still high: respectively, 83 and 61 percent).

TABLE 5.7

Percentage of Metros with High, Middle, and Low Rankings for Selected Measures of Employment, Earnings, and Non-earned Income, by Type/Size of Metro Group, 1997 and 1974–97

Metro Type/Size Group	Rank	Distribution of Rankings, 1997 Levels						Distribution of Rankings, 1974–97 Rates of Change						
		Employ./Pop. Ratio	Earnings/Worker	Earnings/Capita	Income/Capita	TP/Capita	DIR/Capita	Total Employ.	Employ./Pop. Ratio	Earnings/Worker	Earnings/Capita	Income/Capita	TP/Capita	DIR/Capita
Nodal >2 million	High	25.0	100.0	100.0	93.8	37.5	75.0	37.5	43.8	68.8	68.8	68.8	18.8	37.5
	Middle	56.3	0.0	0.0	6.3	25.0	25.0	18.8	37.5	25.0	25.0	25.0	31.3	31.3
	Low	18.8	0.0	0.0	0.0	37.5	0.0	43.8	18.8	6.3	6.3	6.3	50.0	31.3
Nodal 1–2 million	High	72.2	83.3	83.3	83.3	22.2	61.0	38.9	44.4	44.4	72.2	50.0	16.7	27.8
	Middle	22.2	16.7	11.1	16.7	27.8	27.8	33.3	38.9	55.6	22.2	44.4	50.0	44.4
	Low	5.6	0.0	5.6	0.0	50.0	11.1	27.8	16.7	0.0	5.6	5.6	33.3	27.8
Nodal 250,000–1 million	High	54.5	36.4	63.6	54.4	27.3	27.3	27.3	50.0	40.9	50.0	50.0	27.3	40.9
	Middle	40.9	59.1	31.8	40.9	27.3	54.5	54.5	40.9	40.9	45.5	40.9	45.5	40.9
	Low	4.5	4.5	4.5	4.5	45.5	18.2	18.2	9.1	18.2	4.5	9.1	27.3	18.2
Nodal <250,000	High	46.9	9.4	28.1	25.0	18.8	31.3	37.5	46.9	15.6	31.3	21.9	46.9	31.3
	Middle	28.1	40.6	43.8	46.9	31.3	40.6	40.6	21.9	28.1	28.1	40.6	12.5	28.1
	Low	25.0	50.0	28.1	28.1	50.3	28.1	21.9	31.3	56.3	40.6	37.5	40.6	40.6
Functional Nodal >250,000	High	35.3	64.7	70.6	64.7	35.3	52.9	5.9	17.6	52.9	41.2	41.2	41.2	35.3
	Middle	35.3	35.3	29.4	35.3	35.3	35.3	35.3	58.8	11.8	41.2	41.2	29.4	41.2
	Low	29.4	0.0	0.0	0.0	29.4	11.8	58.8	23.6	35.3	17.6	17.6	29.4	23.5
Manufactg./Service >250,000	High	16.7	58.3	25.0	33.3	58.3	33.3	25.0	25.0	41.7	33.3	33.3	33.3	41.7
	Middle	25.0	33.3	50.0	41.7	33.3	33.3	8.3	16.7	41.7	33.3	33.3	41.7	25.0
	Low	58.3	8.3	25.0	25.0	8.3	33.3	66.7	58.3	16.7	33.3	33.3	25.0	33.3
Manufactg./Service <250,000	High	22.7	13.6	4.5	6.8	36.4	11.4	11.4	29.5	13.6	15.9	22.7	31.8	36.4
	Middle	36.4	29.5	31.8	18.2	40.9	31.8	36.4	43.2	38.6	45.5	43.2	47.7	29.5
	Low	40.9	56.8	63.6	75.0	22.7	56.8	52.3	27.3	47.7	38.8	34.1	20.5	34.1
Manufacturing >250,000	High	13.6	50.0	36.4	22.7	27.3	27.3	4.5	9.1	40.9	13.6	18.2	36.4	36.4
	Middle	31.8	45.5	50.0	68.2	31.8	45.5	36.4	36.4	22.7	36.4	27.3	36.4	36.4
	Low	54.5	4.5	13.6	9.1	40.9	27.3	59.1	54.5	36.4	50.0	54.5	13.6	27.3

TABLE 5.7 (continued)

Metro Type/Size Group	Rank	Distribution of Rankings, 1997 Levels						Distribution of Rankings, 1974–97 Rates of Change						
		Employ./Pop. Ratio	Earnings/Worker	Earnings/Capita	Income/Capita	TP/Capita	DIR/Capita	Total Employ.	Employ./Pop. Ratio	Earnings/Worker	Earnings/Capita	Income/Capita	TP/Capita	DIR/Capita
Government/Service > 250,000	High	27.3	30.3	30.3	33.3	27.3	33.3	48.5	33.3	33.3	36.4	30.3	21.2	30.3
	Middle	30.3	39.4	33.3	33.3	45.5	27.3	39.4	42.4	30.3	27.3	30.3	30.3	27.3
	Low	42.4	30.3	36.4	33.3	27.3	39.4	12.1	24.2	36.4	36.4	39.4	43.5	42.4
Government/Service < 250,000	High	51.7	10.3	17.2	13.8	10.3	34.5	55.2	62.1	27.6	51.7	51.7	34.5	37.9
	Middle	31.0	27.6	55.2	48.9	34.5	31.0	24.1	20.7	34.5	24.1	20.7	24.1	31.0
	Low	17.2	62.1	27.6	37.9	55.2	34.5	20.7	17.2	37.9	24.1	27.6	41.4	31.0
Government/Military > 250,000	High	12.5	25.0	6.3	12.5	31.3	12.5	31.3	6.3	43.8	18.8	25.0	37.5	50.0
	Middle	56.3	37.5	56.3	43.8	56.3	25.0	56.3	31.3	43.8	50.0	31.3	37.5	18.8
	Low	31.3	37.5	37.5	43.8	12.5	62.5	12.5	62.5	12.5	31.3	43.8	25.0	31.3
Government/Military < 250,000	High	14.3	4.8	0.0	0.0	52.4	0.0	19.0	14.3	19.0	0.0	14.3	57.1	23.8
	Middle	28.6	9.5	4.8	14.3	28.6	33.3	42.9	23.8	33.3	28.6	28.6	33.3	38.1
	Low	57.1	85.7	95.2	85.7	19.0	66.7	38.1	61.9	47.6	71.4	57.1	9.5	38.1
Resort/Retirement > 250,000	High	23.1	38.5	30.8	61.5	69.3	69.2	84.6	23.1	38.5	38.5	30.8	7.7	15.4
	Middle	23.1	53.8	30.8	15.4	23.2	15.4	15.4	38.5	53.8	30.8	38.5	23.2	38.5
	Low	53.8	7.7	38.5	23.1	7.7	15.4	0.0	38.5	7.7	30.8	30.8	69.2	46.2
Resort/Retirement < 250,000	High	33.3	16.7	16.7	41.7	65.7	58.3	91.7	41.7	41.7	33.3	50.0	33.3	33.3
	Middle	25.0	33.3	25.0	18.7	8.3	33.3	0.0	25.0	16.8	16.7	16.7	16.7	33.3
	Low	41.7	50.0	58.3	41.7	25.0	8.3	8.3	33.3	41.7	50.0	33.3	50.0	33.3

Notes: All metros were ranked from highest to lowest for each of the measures shown. Each metro was classified according to whether its rank fell within the highest, middle, or lowest third of the array. Percentages were then calculated for the number of metros falling within the high, middle, and low classifications. Percentages add to 100, except for rounding.

a. TP is Transfer Payments.

b. DIR is Dividends, Interest, and Rent.

Source: U.S. Bureau of Economic Analysis.

TABLE 5.8

Percentage of Metros with High, Middle, and Low Rankings for Rates of Change of Selected Measures of Employment, Earnings, and Non-earned Income, 1990–97

Metro Type/Size Group		Rank	Distribution of Rankings, 1990–97 Rates of Change						
			Total Employment	Employment/ Population Ratio	Earnings per Worker	Earnings per Capita	Income per Capita	Transfer Payment per Capita	Dividends, Interest, and Rent Payment per Capita
Nodal	> 2 million	High	25.0	0.0	62.5	50.0	43.8	31.3	25.0
		Middle	6.3	50.0	25.0	25.0	31.3	37.5	50.0
		Low	68.8	50.0	12.5	25.0	25.0	31.3	25.0
Nodal	1–2 million	High	27.8	22.2	77.8	55.6	50.0	27.8	38.9
		Middle	33.3	44.4	16.7	38.9	38.9	16.7	44.4
		Low	38.9	33.3	5.6	5.6	11.1	55.6	16.7
Nodal	250,000–1 million	High	36.4	36.4	50.0	63.6	50.0	27.3	40.9
		Middle	45.5	45.5	31.8	22.7	36.4	59.1	40.9
		Low	18.2	18.2	18.2	13.6	13.6	13.6	18.2
Nodal	< 250,000	High	59.4	68.8	31.3	53.1	46.9	40.6	25.0
		Middle	34.4	21.9	37.5	28.1	40.6	12.5	43.8
		Low	6.3	9.4	31.3	18.8	12.5	46.9	31.3
Functional Nodal	> 250,000	High	5.9	29.4	58.8	23.5	17.6	23.5	47.1
		Middle	47.1	29.4	29.4	58.8	52.9	23.5	17.6
		Low	47.1	41.2	11.8	17.6	29.4	52.9	35.3
Manufactg./Service	> 250,000	High	8.3	33.3	25.0	25.0	25.0	41.7	16.7
		Middle	33.3	8.3	25.0	25.0	25.0	50.0	25.0
		Low	58.3	58.3	50.0	50.0	50.0	8.3	58.3
Manufactg./Service	< 250,000	High	25.0	36.4	18.2	27.3	31.8	31.8	27.3
		Middle	31.8	47.7	31.8	29.5	29.5	50.0	29.5
		Low	43.2	15.9	50.0	43.2	38.6	18.2	43.2

TABLE 5.8 (continued)

Distribution of Rankings, 1990–97 Rates of Change

Metro Type/Size Group	Rank	Total Employment	Employment/ Population Ratio	Earnings per Worker	Earnings per Capita	Income per Capita	Transfer Payment per Capita	Dividends, Interest, and Rent Payment per Capita
Manufacturing > 250,000	High	18.2	22.7	27.3	9.1	18.2	27.3	22.7
	Middle	18.2	45.5	45.5	59.1	45.5	18.2	40.9
	Low	63.6	31.8	27.3	31.8	36.4	54.5	36.4
Government/Service > 250,000	High	42.4	24.2	33.3	24.2	27.3	33.3	30.3
	Middle	30.3	30.3	27.3	33.3	27.3	21.2	30.3
	Low	27.3	45.5	39.4	42.4	45.5	45.5	39.4
Government/Service < 250,000	High	55.2	55.2	10.3	44.8	48.3	44.8	58.6
	Middle	31.0	24.1	51.7	31.0	27.6	27.6	27.6
	Low	13.8	20.7	37.9	24.1	24.1	27.6	13.8
Government/Military > 250,000	High	31.3	18.8	37.5	31.3	31.3	31.3	50.0
	Middle	37.5	31.3	43.8	18.8	18.8	43.8	31.3
	Low	31.3	50.0	18.8	50.0	50.0	25.0	18.8
Government/Military < 250,000	High	19.0	38.1	9.5	14.3	33.3	47.6	42.9
	Middle	57.1	23.8	38.1	33.3	38.1	28.6	28.6
	Low	23.8	38.1	52.4	52.4	28.6	23.8	28.6
Resort/Retirement > 250,000	High	46.2	7.7	38.5	7.7	7.7	23.1	7.7
	Middle	30.8	15.4	30.8	46.2	30.8	46.2	30.8
	Low	23.1	76.9	30.8	46.2	61.5	30.8	61.5
Resort/Retirement < 250,000	High	58.3	8.3	16.7	25.0	16.7	33.3	16.7
	Middle	33.3	41.7	25.0	16.7	8.3	33.3	33.3
	Low	8.3	50.0	58.3	58.3	75.0	33.3	50.0

Notes: All metros were ranked from highest to lowest for each of the measures shown. Each metro was classified according to whether its rank fell within the highest, middle, or lowest third of the array. Percentages were then calculated for the number of metros falling within the high, middle, and low classifications. Percentages add to 100, except for rounding.

Source: U.S. Bureau of Economic Analysis.

For this size group—as well as for the very largest—there was considerable variation among metros in growth rates. Five among the 18 (28 percent) were ranked in the top growth bracket (Charlotte, Denver, Fort Worth, Portland–Vancouver, and Salt Lake City) during the most recent period (see table 5.8).

Nodal places with 250,000 to 1 million population tended to rank well for E/P ratios (54 percent are in the top third) and income per capita (54 percent) in 1997 relative to the smaller-size nodal places and most of the non-nodal size/type groups, but fell behind the larger nodal places. Employment growth was favorable (i.e., top ranked) for less than a third of these 22 places during the entire 1974–97 period, however.

Although the 1997 standings of the smallest-size nodal group (with less than 250,000 population) were generally less favorable than those of the other nodal groups, during the 1990s many of these metros showed a sharp improvement in employment growth (see table 5.8). What is striking about the 19 places (59 percent) ranked among the top third for employment growth from 1990 to 1997 is that—unlike the larger nodal groups, of which the fastest-growing places were located almost entirely in the South and West—these faster-growing small nodal places were widely dispersed around the country:

> Amarillo, TX
> Billings, MT
> Bloomington, IN
> Boise City, ID
> Cedar Rapids, IA
> Fargo-Morehead, ND
> Green Bay, WI
> Houma, LA
> La Crosse, WI-MI
> Lafayette, LA
> Lake Charles, LA
> Laredo, TX
> Medford-Ashland, OR
> Ocala, FL
> Saint Cloud, MN
> Sioux Falls, SD
> Tyler, TX
> Victoria, TX
> Yola, CA

Manufacturing-Oriented Groups

Among the manufacturing-oriented groups, the functional nodal group (with 250,000 or more population) showed the highest percentages of metros in the top third for levels of 1997 earnings per worker, earnings per capita, income per capita, and DIR per capita. Yet only 6 percent of these functional nodal metros ranked within the highest third for growth for the entire 1974–97 period. In short, this group has shown poor growth but has maintained relatively high levels of earned and non-earned income.

The remaining three groups of manufacturing-oriented places—manufacturing/service (250,000 or more population), manufacturing/service (less than 250,000 population), and manufacturing metros (250,000 or more population)—show common tendencies for low 1974–97 employment growth and low 1997 E/P ratios. Among the small-size manufacturing/service group, fewer than 7 percent of metros are ranked within the top third ("high") for income per capita. Among the other two groups, the rankings were somewhat more favorable (33 and 23 percent).

Government/Service Metros

The government/service metros, taken as a group, are (next to the resort/retirement metros) the fastest growing within the system. Their E/P ratios vary widely, but there was sharp improvement in these ratios during the 1974–97 period among the smaller metros. Earnings levels vary widely among the larger-size group but are generally moderate to low among the smaller-size group.

Government/Military Metros

The larger government/military places were somewhat more successful than their smaller-size counterparts in rates of growth from 1974 to 1997 in employment, although less than a third of these metros were ranked high. Neither group did well in attaining favorable earnings per worker or income per capita, although the larger-size group did somewhat better. In general, the small-size places appear to rank among the least successful groups of metros in levels of earnings, in income per capita, and in rates of growth of employment and income.

Resort/Retirement Metros

Both size groups of resort/retirement metros are characterized by high rates of employment growth. They are also characterized by relatively high levels of non-earned income. Earnings levels in 1997 were relatively low for the smaller-size group, with 50 percent of places ranked among the bottom third for earnings per worker.

Notes

1. As indicated in appendix A, a lack of adequate data limited the use of these measures to metros with populations of 250,000 or more.

2. The analysis in this and the remainder of this section is based on table 5.2.

3. Unlike the preceding section, which was based on *County Business Patterns* data (except for government sectors), the present section is based on U.S. Bureau of Economic Analysis data (see appendix A).

4. Edward N. Wolff, *Top heavy: A study of the increasing inequality of wealth in America* (New York: Twentieth Century Fund Press, 1995).

5. Actually, only 302 metros were ranked (including the 2 metros not in the continental United States). Nineteen metros were omitted because of incomplete data.

6

Concluding Observations

Major Shifts in Employment Composition

A review of the analysis of the preceding chapters gives rise to five general observations. The first is that the rapid growth of employment in a number of service categories—along with a decline in the importance of goods production as a source of jobs—has brought about major shifts in the industrial composition of employment across a broad spectrum of metropolitan economies.

Generally Stable Metro Specialization

The second observation is that—paradoxically—this transformation of employment composition seems to have done little to alter the fundamental pattern of specialization among many metropolitan economies within the overall system. The evidence for this relative stability of specialization is found by comparing 1997 with 1974 location quotients of major industrial categories in each type/size metro group. What we find, in general, is that the larger nodal places mostly have retained their relative specialization in financial, commercial, and corporate administrative services and in nonprofit services—even while the rapid growth of service employment was a major trend throughout the national economy.

A closer look at these large metros reveals that, although they generally have retained their roles of economic leadership, some have fared better than others. A comparison of other leading large, diversified service centers with New York indicates that a number of these places (including Atlanta, Boston, Dallas, and San Francisco) have strengthened their roles within the metropolitan system. At the same time, New York—while maintaining its position as the preeminent metropolitan economy and increasing its role as a financial center and the leading provider of investment services—may have given ground as a general exporter of corporate services.

113

Among the slow-growing manufacturing-oriented metros, the larger functional nodal places have tended to retain their specialization in manufacturing and administration/auxiliary, and the larger manufacturing/service places in manufacturing and nonprofit services. The manufacturing and smaller manufacturing/service metros were extremely slow growing for the most part and experienced only limited shifts toward greater specialization in service activities (limited largely to nonprofit services). Taken as a whole, it is difficult to find evidence that these slow-growing manufacturing-oriented places were able to develop important new sources of export-based employment and income.

Many of the government/service places, however, did experience high levels of growth and apparently were able to develop effectively, largely within the economic environment of expanding state government and educational and medical institutions (with only limited tendencies toward wider diversification of services).

Among the government/military metros, two of the largest, San Diego and San Antonio, show signs of developing more broadly as service centers. None of the remaining government/military places, however, appears to have achieved significant specialization (as indicated by location quotients), except in federal government and military employment.

The resort/retirement places clearly experienced their very high levels of growth as a result of forces favoring shifts of retired populations toward amenity-rich metros (especially those located in semitropical Florida), along with the attraction of vacationers and resort-oriented transients. These places have maintained high levels of specialization in retailing, consumer services, and FIRE agents and brokers. The last specialization, however, is apparently oriented to servicing a consumer market. Two of this group of metros, Fort Lauderdale and Tampa, show signs of becoming diversified service centers.

Earnings Relatives and Nodal Metro Specialization

The third observation is that measures of earnings relatives—which relate earnings per worker in the various industries to earnings levels of unskilled workers—indicate that very large nodal metros are indeed the most specialized in financial and business/professional services, and that levels of specialization in these services (as reflected in earnings relatives) have risen. They also show that functional nodal places are characterized by relatively high earnings relatives in a number of industrial categories, presumably reflecting high average levels of skill and experience.

Export-Base Problems in Some Metros

The fourth observation is that the failure of many manufacturing-oriented and government/military places to develop significant new export bases during a period in which they suffered an erosion of their goods-production sectors raises questions as to how employment growth—even at a very slow pace—has been achieved. Urban economies do not grow by "taking in their own washing." The export-base idea is essentially a truism: Because urban places import a variety of goods and services, there must be an inflow of export-generated income or of its equivalent (non-earned income flows).

There is good reason to hold that a considerable amount of import substitution has been accomplished through the widespread growth of services. Certainly, a greater proportion of so-phisticated medical services was performed in local hospitals in 1997 than in 1974. Similarly, no doubt, the percentages of post–high school courses offered locally increased, and a larger share of a variety of fairly unsophisticated business and professional services was performed within the local metropolitan economy. Yet there appears to be little reason to suspect that the volume of imports diminished or that increases in import substitution could have been suffi-cient to sustain the weaker metropolitan economies in the face of declining goods production.

Growing Non-Earned Income

My own judgment is that we cannot begin to understand the fundamental economics of metro-politan growth and change without extending the analysis to take into account the greatly in-creased role of non-earned income. This leads to the fifth observation: Non-earned income (DIR and TP) has grown to levels that account for very significant shares of total personal income.

These non-earned flows have grown in importance everywhere, but it seems clear that their growth has given rise to increased inequality among metropolitan economies. Within the U.S. metropolitan system, some places have benefited more than others. This is true not only because of migrations by senior citizens (who take their portable Social Security, Medicare, and investment income to Southern and Western spas), but also because some types of metros are more important centers of personal wealth than others. Moreover, the increasing importance of DIR as a source of personal income is itself an indication of increasing inequality of income among individuals within metropolitan economies.

In any event, non-earned income clearly has come to play a larger role in all metropolitan economies than formerly. To the extent that marginal metros—especially overspecialized manu-facturing places—have been able to eke out low levels of employment growth, increasing non-earned income flows in all likelihood have played a part.

APPENDIX A

Notes on Definitions, Data, and Problems of Analysis

This is a study of changes in the industrial composition, earnings structure, and growth characteristics of U.S. metropolitan statistical areas based on data for 1974, 1990, and 1997. Some key points regarding the selection and processing of these data are sketched below.

Defining the Metropolitan Area

The term "metropolitan area" is used throughout to refer to these categories defined by the U.S. Bureau of the Census: Primary Metropolitan Statistical Area (PMSA), Metropolitan Statistical Area (MSA), and New England County Metropolitan Area (NECMA). A PMSA is a metropolitan area that is part of a Consolidated Metropolitan Statistical Area (CMSA), whereas an MSA is not.[1] Both MSAs and PMSAs are intended to approximate metropolitan economies in which there is usually at least one city of 50,000 persons and in which there is a minimum of commuter inflow or outflow. PMSAs, MSAs, and NECMAs consist of one or more counties, and employment and earnings data accordingly are a consolidation of county data. NECMAs provide an approximation of metropolitan areas in the New England states, where MSAs are defined in terms of cities and towns.

Constituent counties of PMSAs, MSAs, and NECMAs conform to the Bureau of the Census's June 1990 definition.[2] This definition was used for each of the years studied, and metropolitan areas accordingly are comparable throughout.

The Data

The primary data sources were *County Business Patterns* (*CBP;* issued by the Bureau of the Census) computer tapes and disks, and U.S. Bureau of Economic Analysis CD-ROM (Regional Economic Information System) files. *CBP* provides county employment and earnings data at a detailed SIC level for a given week in March of each year, but only for nonfarm, nongovernment employment, and it makes no estimate of self-employment. The BEA provides annual county employment and earnings data for farm, nonfarm, and government employment on a much less detailed SIC basis, but it does estimate self-employment. In the analysis of industry employment and earnings, the detailed *CBP* data (which, as noted above, include only nongovernment employment) have been combined with comparable BEA data for government employment, with government broken down under three headings: federal, military, and state and local. In preparing earnings estimates for the three government categories, the BEA earnings data—which are annual totals—have been adjusted to a weekly level comparable to *CBP* earnings. However, it must be noted that, throughout the study, BEA estimates were used where the analysis is of *total* metropolitan employment and earned or non-earned income.

Industry Groups Analyzed

The industry groups and subgroups analyzed in the study are the ones shown in table 1.3. Although no subgroups of mining, construction, manufacturing, wholesaling, and retailing are examined, two subgroups of transportation, communications, and utilities, and three subgroups of FIRE were broken out, as were three major subgroups of the large heterogeneous "services" classification: business/professional, nonprofit, and consumer. The nonprofit service classification was further broken down into health services, education services, and social/organization services. SIC codes for component classes of FIRE, business/professional services, and nonprofit services are presented in appendix B. As noted above, the government category was subdivided into three groups: federal, military, and state and local.

Two special problems that were encountered in compiling and analyzing the data deserve special mention. The first relates to the business/professional services category. Ideally, this category would be examined in greater detail, because many of these services experienced a very high rate of growth during the 1974–90 period and are of special interest. Unfortunately, important changes in SIC definitions were instituted in 1987, with the result that the combinations of SICs shown in appendix B were necessary to devise categories inclusive enough to be comparable for the years under study.

The second problem relates to the category state and local government. This category includes state and municipal government workers along with state and local educational institutions. Privately operated educational institutions, however, are classified under educational services. This makes it more difficult to assess the significance of changes in the employment levels of these services than would be the case if they were more clearly delineated. The problem does not appear to be serious in the case of health services, because government-supported hospitals are reported under health services. State university and college employment and earnings do pose a problem, however, because they account for a significant share of employment in higher education and yet are lumped with government employment under state and local government.

Dealing with Data Omissions in the CBP Material

Anyone who uses the *CBP* employment data for detailed economic analysis faces a problem: Regulations restrict the publication of employment data for a given SIC when there are so few enterprises in a given county that the employment level of a single enterprise possibly could be estimated from such published data. Where such a possibility exists, the data are suppressed, and a code letter is shown for the appropriate (usually 3-digit) SIC indicating the range of values within which the true value lies: a, 0–19; b, 20–99; c, 100–249; d, 250–499; e, 250–499; f, 500–999; g, 1,000–2,499; h, 2,500–4,999; i, 5,000–9,999; j, 10,000–24,999; k, 25,000–49,999; and l, 50,000–99,999.

To estimate suppressed data, the computer was programmed to substitute mid-values for all letter codes and to further adjust by increasing or decreasing all estimates within a broad (usually 2-digit) SIC, until combined data (both known and estimated) equaled the known published employment within that SIC. Because there were virtually no suppressions of data at the 2-digit SIC level (and because data were for the most part suppressed only for small counties and for relatively unimportant SICs), this method of adjustment appears to have been quite satisfactory.

Data suppression was a more serious problem in compiling earnings. Earnings data are suppressed in every instance in which employment data are suppressed, but no code letters are published to indicate the range of values of missing earnings data, which makes it impossible to estimate them directly. A method was devised by which earnings per worker were computed from known earnings and employment data, and these computations were used to estimate the missing earnings information.

Earnings data were reasonably reliable for the larger metros, but estimation proved less satisfactory for smaller places. Accordingly, earnings were analyzed only for metros with a 1990 population of more than 250,000.

Classifying Metros

In classifying metros by major types, a clustering algorithm was used to group places on the basis of similarities in the industrial composition of their employment. The statistical information processed consisted of the Z scores of the location quotients of employment in major industrial categories for each metro. The clustering algorithm proceeds by measuring the squared Euclidian distance between pairs of metros in an iterative process that results in breaking out groups of similar metros.[3] This analysis was carried out separately for metros with a population of 250,000 or more and for those with less than 250,000, to take account (at least partially) of the effects of size on industrial specialization (see chapter 2).

Metros within clusters were then examined by comparing location quotients to determine those similarities of composition that had been picked up by the statistical clustering procedure.

This analysis revealed that metros with more than 250,000 population fell into four general categories:

1. *Diversified service centers* (i.e., nodal), metros with characteristics described in chapter 2. This group appeared to be the most homogeneous, with most metros falling within a single cluster.
2. *Government-oriented places*, metros with relatively large shares of employment falling within the general industrial category "government."
3. *Manufacturing-oriented places*, those with high manufacturing location quotients.
4. *Resort/retirement places*, characterized generally by high location quotients for retailing and consumer services. Places in this latter category fell largely within a single cluster, but the two gambling centers with more than 250,000 population, Las Vegas and Atlantic City, formed a separate cluster.

By careful analysis of detailed location quotients of these larger metros, the government-oriented metros could be broken down into two groups: those with large shares of state and local (and sometimes federal) government employment, the *government/service metros*; and those with large shares of military and (usually) federal government employment, the *government/military metros*.

The manufacturing-oriented metros fell into three groups: *functional nodals*, distinguished principally by relatively large shares of employment in manufacturing and administration/auxiliary; *manufacturing/service*, distinguished principally by large shares of employment in manufacturing and in nonprofit services; and *manufacturing*, distinguished by large shares of employment in manufacturing but not in business or nonprofit services. Typically, location quotients in retailing in this last group were high.

Among the metros with less than 250,000 population, the results of the analysis were similar, but patterns of specialization tended to be somewhat less well articulated. This was especially true in the case of nodal metros. These smaller nodal metros were for the most part distinguished by high location quotients in wholesaling. The smaller manufacturing-oriented places fell largely into the manufacturing/service category, characterized by above-average location quotients in nonprofit services as well as in manufacturing. Relatively few of these smaller manufacturing-oriented places could be classified as functional nodal or manufacturing.

Government-oriented metros, once identified by cluster analysis, were found to fall into the two classes: government/service, which tend to be specialized as state capitals and/or the sites of state-operated universities and medical centers; and government/military, which have military or other government installations. The remaining metros with less than 250,000 population were resort/retirement metros, heavily specialized as resorts or as meccas for retired persons.

Preparing the Indexes of Earnings Relatives

Earnings relatives were computed for each metro with a population of 250,000 or more. The computation was done by dividing earnings per worker (adjusted for average weekly hours) in each industry category by earnings per worker (adjusted for average weekly hours) in the eating-drinking industrial subcategory (SIC 58). Sources of data for employment and weekly earnings and methods of estimation are explained above. The data for average weekly hours for all nongovernment employees (which were used to adjust earnings per worker) were obtained for 1974, 1990, and 1990 from table C-L, U.S. Bureau of Labor Statistics, *Employment and Earnings*, Table C2, March 1975, March 1991, and 1997 issues. Average hours data for government workers are unpublished and were obtained directly from *Current Population Studies*.

Notes

1. A CMSA is an approximation of a major metropolitan region, such as Greater New York. CMSA data are not analyzed in this study.

2. See Appendix II, *Statistical Abstract of the United States* (Washington, DC: U.S. Government Printing Office, 1991).

3. The process uses the Horizontal Icicle Plot Program Using Complete Linkage, Hierarchical Cluster Analysis (part of the Statistical Package for the Social Sciences, or SPSS).

APPENDIX B

Component SIC Codes for FIRE, Business/Professional Services, Nonprofit Services, and Consumer Services

---

FINANCE, INSURANCE, AND REAL ESTATE (FIRE)

SIC Code   *Title*

Banking (60 + 61)

SIC Code	Title
6000	Depository institutions
6010	Central reserve depository
6020	Commercial banks
6030	Savings institutions
6060	Credit unions
6080	Foreign banks and branches and agencies
6090	Functions closely related to banking
6100	Nondepository institutions
6110	Federal and federally sponsored credit institutions
6140	Personal credit institutions
6150	Business credit institutions
6160	Mortgage bankers and brokers

Insurance Carriers (63)

SIC Code	Title
6300	Insurance carriers
6310	Life insurance
6320	Medical service and health insurance
6321	Accident and health insurance
6324	Hospital and medical service plans
6330	Fire, marine, and casualty insurance
6350	Surety insurance
6360	Title insurance

6370   Pension, health, and welfare funds
6390   Insurance carriers, n.e.c.[a]

FIRE Agents and Brokers (62 + 64 + 65 + 67)

6200   Security and commodity brokers
6210   Security brokers and dealers
6220   Commodity and contract brokers, and dealers
6230   Security and commodity exchanges
6280   Security and commodity services

6400   Insurance agents, brokers, and services

6500   Real estate
6510   Real estate operators and lessors
6530   Real estate agents and managers
6540   Title abstract offices
6550   Subdividers and developers
6552   Subdividers and developers, n.e.c.
6553   Cemetery subdividers and developers

6700   Holding and other investment offices
6710   Holding offices
6720   Investment offices
6730   Trusts
6732   Educational, religious, etc., trusts
6733   Trusts, n.e.c.
6790   Miscellaneous investing
6792   Oil royalty traders
6794   Patent owners and lessors
6798   Real estate investment trusts
6799   Investors, n.e.c.

BUSINESS/PROFESSIONAL SERVICES (73 + 81 + 87)

SIC Code   *Title*

7300   Business services
7310   Advertising
7311   Advertising agencies
7312   Outdoor advertising services
7313   Radio, TV, publisher representatives
7319   Advertising, n.e.c.
7320   Credit reporting and collection
7322   Adjustment and collection services

7323	Credit reporting services
7330	Mailing, reproduction, stenographic
7331	Direct mail advertising services
7334	Photocopying and duplicating services
7335	Commercial photography
7336	Commercial art and graphic design
7338	Secretarial and court reporting
7340	Services to buildings
7342	Disinfecting and pest control services
7349	Building maintenance services, n.e.c.
7350	Miscellaneous equipment rental and leasing
7352	Medical equipment rental
7353	Heavy construction equipment rental
7359	Equipment rental and leasing, n.e.c.
7360	Personnel supply services
7361	Employment agencies
7363	Help supply services
7370	Computer and data processing services
7371	Computer programming services
7372	Prepackaged software
7373	Computer integrated systems design
7374	Data processing and preparation
7375	Information retrieval services
7376	Computer facilities management
7377	Computer rental and leasing
7378	Computer maintenance and repair
7379	Computer related services, n.e.c.
7380	Miscellaneous business services
7381	Detective and armored car services
7382	Security systems services
7383	News syndicate
7384	Photofinishing laboratories
7389	Business services, n.e.c.
8100	Legal services
8700	Engineering and management services
8710	Engineering and architectural services
8711	Engineering services
8712	Architectural services
8713	Surveying services
8720	Accounting, auditing, and bookkeeping
8730	Research and testing services

8731	Commercial physical research
8733	Noncommercial research organizations
8734	Testing laboratories
8740	Management and public relations
8741	Management services
8742	Management consulting services
8743	Public relations services
8744	Facilities support services
8748	Business consulting, n.e.c.

NONPROFIT SERVICES

| SIC Code | Title |

Health Services (80)

8000	Health services
8010	Offices and clinics of medical doctors
8020	Offices and clinics of dentists
8030	Offices of osteopathic physicians
8040	Offices of other health practitioners
8041	Offices and clinics of chiropractors
8042	Offices and clinics of optometrists
8043	Offices and clinics of podiatrists
8049	Offices of health practitioners, n.e.c.
8050	Nursing and personal care facilities
8060	Hospitals
8070	Medical and dental laboratories
8071	Medical laboratories
8072	Dental laboratories
8080	Home health care services
8090	Health and allied services, n.e.c.

Educational Services (82)

(*Note:* Does not include institutions in which workers are on government payrolls.)

8200	Educational services
8210	Elementary and secondary schools
8220	Colleges and universities
8230	Libraries
8240	Vocational schools
8290	Schools and educational services, n.e.c.

Social Services/Organizations (83 + 84 + 86)

8300	Social services
8320	Individual and family services
8330	Job training and related services
8350	Child day care services
8360	Residential care
8390	Social services, n.e.c.
8400	Museums, botanical, zoological gardens
8410	Museums and art galleries
8420	Botanical and zoological gardens
8600	Membership organizations
8610	Business associations
8620	Professional organizations
8630	Labor organizations
8640	Civic and social associations
8650	Political organizations
8660	Religious organizations
8690	Membership organizations, n.e.c.

CONSUMER SERVICES (70 + 72 + 75 + 76 + 78 + 79)

SIC Code	Title
7000	Hotels and other lodging places
7010	Hotels and motels
7020	Rooming and boarding houses
7030	Campus and recreational vehicle parks
7032	Sporting and recreational camps
7033	Trailer parks and campsites
7040	Membership-basis organization hotels
7200	Personal services
7210	Laundry, cleaning, and garment services
7211	Power laundries, family and commercial
7212	Garment pressing and cleaners' agents
7213	Linen supply
7215	Coin-operated laundries and cleaning
7216	Dry-cleaning plants, except rugs
7217	Carpet and upholstery cleaning
7218	Industrial launderers
7219	Laundry and garment services, n.e.c.

7220	Photographic studios, portrait
7230	Beauty shops
7240	Barber shops
7250	Shoe repair and shoeshine parlors
7260	Funeral service and crematories
7290	Miscellaneous personal services
7291	Tax return preparation services
7299	Miscellaneous personal services, n.e.c.
7500	Auto repair, services, and parking
7510	Automotive rentals, no drivers
7513	Truck rental and leasing, no drivers
7514	Passenger car rental
7515	Passenger car leasing
7519	Utility trailer rental
7520	Automobile parking
7530	Automotive repair shops
7532	Top and body repair and paint shops
7533	Auto exhaust system repair shops
7534	Tire retreading and repair shops
7536	Automotive glass replacement shops
7537	Automotive transmission repair shops
7538	General automotive repair shops
7539	Automotive repair shops, n.e.c.
7540	Automotive services, except repairs
7542	Carwashes
7549	Automotive services, n.e.c.
7600	Miscellaneous repair services
7620	Electrical repair shops
7622	Radio and television repair
7623	Refrigeration service and repair
7629	Electrical repair shops, n.e.c.
7630	Watch, clock, and jewelry repair
7640	Reupholstery and furniture repair
7690	Miscellaneous repair shops
7692	Welding repair
7694	Armature rewinding shops
7699	Repair service, n.e.c.
7800	Motion pictures
7810	Motion picture production and services
7812	Motion picture and video production

7819	Services allied to motion pictures
7820	Motion picture distribution and services
7822	Motion picture and tape distribution
7829	Motion picture distribution services
7830	Motion picture theaters
7832	Motion picture theaters, except drive-ins
7833	Drive-in motion picture theaters
7840	Video tape rental
7900	Amusement and recreation services
7910	Dance studios, schools, and halls
7920	Producers, orchestras, entertainers
7922	Theatrical producers and services
7929	Entertainers and entertainment groups
7930	Bowling centers
7940	Commercial sports
7941	Sports clubs, managers, and promoters
7948	Racing, including track operation
7990	Misc. amusement, recreation services
7991	Physical fitness facilities
7992	Public golf courses
7993	Coin-operated amusement devices
7996	Amusement parks
7997	Membership sports and recreation clubs
7999	Amusement and recreation, n.e.c.

Note: a. n.e.c. = not elsewhere classified.